Being Held By God

*How I Caused My Own Miracle
and How You Can Too!*

Nannette Jodar

iUniverse, Inc.
Bloomington

Being Held by God
How I Caused My Own Miracle and How You Can Too!

iUniverse books may be ordered through booksellers or by contacting:

iUniverse
1663 Liberty Drive
Bloomington, IN 47403
www.iuniverse.com
1-800-Authors (1-800-288-4677)

ISBN: 978-1-4502-9365-5 (sc)
ISBN: 978-1-4502-9367-9 (dj)
ISBN: 978-1-4502-9366-2 (ebk)

Printed in the United States of America

iUniverse rev. date: 2/15/2011

Contents

For My Support System

Being Held By God is dedicated to the special friends and family members who have rallied to my physical, spiritual and emotional support during my cancer journey.

My Guide, Jesus. Without whom neither *Being Held By God*, nor I would be existing today. The messages in *Being Held By God* would not be.

Kanelechi Esther Kamah. Without her late evening calls to make sure I was OK; I wouldn't have learned how special Kanelechi had been to me. Without our eventful prayer night, the mountain would not have been moved. Kanelechi is my bosom buddy, confidant, and mountain moving prayer-warrior partner. Together, our prayers to God have moved mountains and created miracles. When we can't pray and talk for a few days our lives seem empty and stalled.

To **Mike**, the man I fell in love with thirteen years ago and love even more today. As my primary caregiver, he made sure I had a home over my head, children and grandchildren to love and who loved me back. He gave me laughter, hugs, and kisses along the scariest part of my journey.

Ruth and her husband, Mike gave their friendship, spiritual, and emotional support. Thank you, Jesus, for Ruth's wisdom.

Sue, my nearest confidant and bosom friend, was with me whenever I needed someone's shoulder to cry on, or a friend to hang out with and laugh; also offered up her prayers for me. One of those best friends you treasure for life.

Michele and Timothy, my sister and brother. My only family I have left. Were there for me every possible time they could from a distance.

Joy gave me her friendship, support and strength with tears.

To all the others, who traveled this journey with me the past three years and continue on this path with me today.

Disclaimer

Diet/Exercise Regimens

You should not undertake any diet/exercise regimen recommended in this book before consulting your personal physician. Neither the author nor the publisher shall be responsible or liable for any loss or damage allegedly arising as a consequence of your use or application of any information or suggestions contained in this book.

I do want to add that if your mission in this lifetime is complete, no effort made to overcome or cure what is wrong with your body will work. When your mission on this earth is over, it is time for you to pass onto the spirit world with God, which is not to be any scarier than being born into this world.

Preface

Many refer to me as a "Walking Miracle", "Miracle Woman", and the "Amazing Woman". This is my story of how I was led to obtaining my miraculous cure from cancer in less than three weeks!

How you can too.

Three years ago I was diagnosed with stage four inflammatory breast cancer which had metastasized to the two upper lobes of my liver and all the surrounding lymph nodes running from my thyroid down around my breast up to my right armpit area. My doctors told me there was no survival or cure and that "this is a life ending event."

Because of the persistence of those who personally knew me and complete strangers, upon hearing parts of my remarkable story of how I overcame this life ending event, I finally gave in to all the pressure from the messengers God sent me. They announced and instructed how important it was for me to get my story out to the public via every available method; especially to write a book about the process leading to my miracle. The behavior of the many people, who insisted I write *Being Held By God*, became a message I would hear frequently. So much so, that as I approached the moment in time of beginning *Being*

Held By God, the demand of sharing my story with the public increased almost daily.

I realized my destiny of the importance of publicly making my story available to others like me and those close to them.

Hopefully you will be inspired and given hope. The primary purpose behind *Being Held By God* is to help you realize it is possible to receive miracles from cancer and many of the other major ailments from which many suffer. I hope also that you will find some emotional support and inspiration from what you will read.

Introduction

For all the gracious Wisconsinites and those who know you.

I grew up in Chilton, Wisconsin. It is exciting and precious to me to be your published author from Chilton, and, as a Wisconsinite, here to help you tap into what is available and out there waiting for you to have better health, but more specifically have a unique relationship with our Creator.

I'm honored to be able to tell you my story of overcoming a horrible, rare and unbeatable type of breast cancer which everyone, including the doctors, completely believed would cause my "life ending event" in 2008, 11 years ago! Let me add, that doctors still in 2019 are shocked to hear that I survived my diagnosis that I always must chuckle (understatement) inside when I see their jaws drop to the floor and their eyes widen! Inflammatory breast cancer is still today such an extremely rare, impossible to diagnose
type of cancer. To this day, it still has a survival rate of less than 5%, less than 2 years for most survivors, and definitely not longer than 5 to 6 years!

It was God's design for me to return this year with my book, *Being Held By God-How I Caused My Own Miracle and How*

You Can Too! once again and expand on what I did to overcome this type of cancer. Also to satisfy the demand of more information and detail from readers years ago, I've added the *Being Held By God-How I Caused My Own Miracle and How You Can Too! Workbook.*

The point is; if I can do it, so can you. Your body is uniquely designed to heal itself given the right tools to create your perfect health. I'm not only talking about cancer, by the way.

Being Held By God reads as a diary of the events and messengers who led me to the resources God wanted me to use to affect my cure. There is a short chronological timeline in Appendix A and a list of the complimentary therapies (alternative medicine) that I had implemented should you choose to use any one of the same therapies I had used to get my miracle. Some of you might think the material seems a bit on the evangelical side. Some of you might think *Being Held By God* tends towards the metaphysical. Either way, I reported to you what I did, and how God led me to use and do the therapies I used. I gave you the information; it's up to you to choose how to implement any of it, or all of it, for you and your family or friends.

God is my confidant, my protector and business partner, whom I will be calling "Jesus" or "God" in *Being Held By God*. You may call him God, your higher self, the universe, divine, intelligent designer or whatever seems to help you tap into the spirit of your soul and your relationship with our creator or Intelligent Designer. But I will use "Jesus" or "God" most of the time, because that is who my primary relationship is with and has been with over the years. Visualizing Jesus made our relationship more personal and real for me. Jesus is my primary personal guide with his angels. He is always around me. So, if you are not Christian, please do not let my personal relationship with Jesus make you not read *Being Held By God*.

The message and perfect health is for everyone.

The story within is what it is. I wrote it in a way to try to provide you with a relationship with me, and to help you understand the severity of the cancer with which I was diagnosed. Then finally, the impact of the speed at which the cancer was gone once I listened to God and His messengers He sent my way. One of my oncologists referred to my diagnosis as the "worst of the worst of the worst type of cancer anyone could ever be diagnosed with!"

God led me to the resources He did, which caused my events to have been different than they were predicted to be by all the cancer statistics. Which by the way, according to both of my oncologists; I had totally blown away all the numbers for the type of cancer I had been diagnosed along with the numbers for cancer in general. As a result, I am blazing my own clinical trial, my own path. The doctors don't know what to anticipate as the next step for me anymore.

If it hadn't been for the fact that I knew with all of my heart and soul that God had plans for me, there would not have been the miracle. If I had not listened to His messengers, and if I had not opened my heart and mind to the messages He sent me throughout this whole journey, there would not have been this miracle; nor *Being Held By God* to help you.

I learned to let God into my life during that part of my journey more than I did previously. I began to allow Him to be my lead in our dance together and to let Him guide me in everything I do and say. Consequently, He had sent me to help you learn how to create your own miracles. How what I did can help you to overcome cancer, and some of the other major disorders of our bodies by implementing one or all of the types of therapies I've listed in the back of *Being Held By God*, as well as within the story.

After reading *Being Held By God*, search for local similar complimentary therapies and willing staff of the medical community to do what you believe and know is right for your body's miracle and health, or use the same sources as I had used. Listen for God to show you the way.

The complimentary therapies I've used tremendously helped me to tolerate the six chemo times I still did after the miracle and kept me looking very healthy and fantastic during the chemo. My personally designed cancer cure program reduced the cancer treatment process expected for me to only six chemo treatments, which ended when all the tests showed a resolution of all the cancer.

I do want to add that if your mission in this lifetime is complete, no effort made to overcome or cure what is wrong with your body will work. When your mission on this earth is over it is time for you to pass onto the spirit world with God, which is not to be any scarier than being born into this world.

Enjoy *Being Held By God*, and I wish you all the miracles you desire.

Dance With Jesus!

Nannette

Chapter One

Walking Miracle

Wow! How excited can a person get?! My dance routine with God changed from being held at a local club to outside the ballroom on the beach with my prince charming!

Three years ago I went from having been diagnosed with the rarest, most impossible to beat, difficult to diagnose and the worst of the worst combination of cancer after a period of four months of medical tests, doctors and exams to being given a miracle cure in less than three weeks! You see, I was supposed to have died in 2008 from stage four inflammatory breast cancer which had spread to the top two lobes of my liver and all the surrounding lymph nodes.

Life expectancy from a diagnosis of the extremely aggressive inflammatory breast cancer alone, regardless of the stage someone is in, is significantly less than ten percent. Add into my diagnosis the liver had been metastasized as well as the lymph nodes in the area towards my thyroid. I was told my diagnosis was a "life ending event" and that there would be no survival or cure! The life ending event should have occurred very rapidly; within a few months, yet, here I am three years later. Alive, extremely healthy, cancer free and my life had been drastically changed.

My life changed from a quiet life with Mike, and his and my kids, our grandkids, and both of us working and expecting to work beyond the normal retirement age to where Mike and I no longer share our lives. My life had further transformed from being told I would die, to having wrote *Being Held By God,* organized three non-profits; one called Cancer Survivor Hands 4 Hope to assist other survivors restart their lives after cancer, the second nonprofit, Watermark College Planning Foundation, coaches and educates college bound families through the college entry process, and the third non-profit, Retrieving Family Values and Enlightenment Core Services helps individuals that are unemployed without skills become viable and skilled employees. In addition to being involved with these non-profits, I had been invited to become involved with a Nigerian dignitary's numerous humanitarian projects in Nigeria with and without the above non-profits. Life had certainly turned around to an abundance of interesting life events since the cancer.

In spite of my phenomenal reinvention, I am still trying to grasp the severity of the potential this virus (cancer) could have had against my life and its quality. Add into the mixture the amazement and beauty of the miracle I had been given by my prince charming.

Getting rid of the cancer was so extremely simple! I am still impressed with how easy and simplistic it was to blow away my diagnosis!

In less than three weeks after I took steps to manage my own health, the tumorous *hot spots* were gone! After I implemented the counsel of an herbalist, changed my diet, prayer by people all over the country, and believed that I was being guided towards my course of a cure, I was able to astound my doctors with the disappearance of the tumors. My doctors had been left with no clinical trials or other cancer statistics for them to be guided with how to anticipate any direction of medical care for me. To this day I am still my own clinical trial, my own medical path. The course of action I had taken changed my "life ending event" to one of survival and an inspiration to others suffering from cancer and many other major disorders. Many of these persons, who had incorporated the skills of the same herbalist, changed their diet and added prayer, are also cancer free today.

To having been put in the position of being called a "walking miracle" by so many, whether they just met me or knew me before the beginning of my journey still sends shivers of amazement. I still wonder why me? Disbelief, because I never thought I'd be selected to experience a miracle! Why would God make *me*, Nannette, a "walking miracle"? Never thought I would ever personally be involved with overcoming cancer because no other family member ever had cancer; none that I knew of before I was diagnosed. Cancer was the furthest from my mind. Why was I chosen to bear the dramatic experience of a miracle from cancer? And why did it have to immediately be stage four inflammatory breast cancer, of all types?

There are so many others out there that seemed to be more deserving of a miracle. After all there was nothing eventful or significant happening in my life. Being the recipient of such a phenomenal cure and miracle was more than I took the time to grasp. I didn't think that I had been anything near a miracle! I was just Nannette; who worked hard every day as a financial planner trying to survive daily life to keep my life intact. Not any different from anyone else out there who worked hard each day and had bills to pay, family to care for and love, and friends to spend fun times with when we got together.

I wasn't any greatly knowledgeable Christian. I couldn't even name the books in the bible, if you asked me. I believed in God, prayed periodically, occasionally asked God to do favors for me or someone else, and attended church when it was convenient or felt a need to be there. I had my moments of temper or intolerance, as well as being unable to offer forgiveness to some people. So by no means was I a perfect person to receive a miracle!

In fact, it took quite some time to fathom what people were telling me as they heard my story, because it hadn't occurred to me that I was a miracle when all I did was follow the instructions of the herbalist to change around Mike's and my eating habits, take the supplements she recommended for me, practiced some meditative activities, implemented some other alternative therapies and changed some of my attitudes towards myself and others.

Why would I think that what I had changed in my life would be considered a miracle? Anyone could have done what I did; and can do it! I'm not discrediting the fact that God had led me to my miracle, which I'm now passing on to you.

I'm trying to help you and I relate what it felt like, as well as help anyone reading *Being Held By God*, that although this event had occurred to me, and is miraculous, it can as easily happen to you. After so many others had called me a miracle, or told me that I received a miracle, was when I began to realize the impact of what had happened to me, and it was during the many following months after the disappearance of the tumors that I began to realize piece by piece the severity of my own cancer!

Maybe not fully understanding the severity of the cancer I was diagnosed with helped me to embark on a mission to find the way to get rid of the cancer, because it caused me to listen more closely to *where and to whom* God led me; therefore it created the miracle. Better still, because I was led to find those resources that I could use to get well; had extended my mission to be passed on to anyone else to use to get healthy.

So here I am, the "Miracle Woman", the "Amazing Woman", and the "Walking Miracle"; as I've been called, telling you my story so you can also get your cure.

As I mentioned, I never thought something such as my story in *Being Held By God* would ever be a reality for me or a part of my history. I fully expected that I would live out my life as the mother of my kids, grandmother, and loving wife. Work until retirement at the age of eighty as a college financial planner and retirement income planner, then die of old age when I got older happy with my family around me surrounded with my *white picket fence*. After all, isn't that what life is to be?

A year ago, as I sat in my bedroom on the bed trying to figure out how to share my miracle and the consequent many blessings showered upon me from above when this journey began. Sitting there, touching the keys on my loyal and reliable laptop of many years; I hoped that my cancer story would be an inspiration to you or help you get your miracle. Others had been inspired with my story to the point of believing it could happen to them or someone they knew. Some have added that my story had caused them to get goose bumps!!

Jesus knew what He was doing when we started this dance together in December 2007. Or, maybe before! Also, without realizing, when the symptoms started back in March of 2008, I was actually getting what I had prayed for, and asked to receive from God. I remember lamenting before God and in my own privacy, for Him to take me Home. I wanted to die in the worst way, being drained and fatigued from everything life had put before me the past forty-something years and I wanted out. Heaven was definitely looking like a better proposition. I wanted to give up, but Jesus knew that there was light in my soul. He must have seen a strong fire there which to me only seemed barely an ember.

So why did I want out?

Why couldn't I see in me what God saw? I couldn't see how my life made a difference to anyone because so many things in it seemed to turn out wrong.

Chapter Two

I Asked God to Die – Take Me Home

I'm going to share with you that I was feeling at a pretty low pith of my being before the transformation started. Maybe, you will feel a companionship with me, maybe not. We both suffered emotional pain of some sort; or are still suffering. For me, life had a lot of wonderful parts to it. Yet, I was going through some very emotional and physical events that were making me more and more sad as 2007 passed in time. I was frustrated and angry with God, myself, and the world. I prayed for our family to be joyful again, for Mike and I to be joyful again, and if not I wanted God to take me home. I was done with life and felt as though I couldn't do anything right or make anyone happy that I cared about. Also, so many things I hoped would turn out didn't and I felt disappointed and rejected.

I felt robbed of a life I had expected to get. My life was supposed to have been the "white picket fence lifestyle" with my husband, kids and grandchildren. So here I am older than I'm going to disclose, looking younger than I am, and feeling that young inside and with many experiences that seemed to get nothing and a body that had begun to refuse to do the things it used to when I was younger.

As my body had begun to malfunction, I suspected it wasn't going to hold up to provide me with another thirty-five plus years of a life I still dreamed of having and accomplishments that I wanted to complete to make my life seem worthwhile. My body, soul, and heart were so drained that it was difficult to effortlessly complete the tasks I used to accomplish while my kids were growing up. Cutting the grass took the whole day with breaks in between or two days to complete. There was only a quarter acre of lawn to cut with an 1800 square-foot ranch home that took up some of that quarter acre. It was a struggle to clean my home in one day! My attitude towards the house and life was that again I had been disappointed with the results. I had emotionally given up; physically fatigued from emotionally fighting to always be the *strong woman, a fighter, the iron woman,* and depicted as the "knight in white armor among a pack of wolves with her blade in its sheath". I was drained of taking care of everything in life by myself, for myself, and everyone else. In the past if I stepped out of my norm to ask someone to help me or do something for me, I felt as though I had extremely burdened them in some way, or the person would expect some sort of compensation for their help, or say they were too busy for me. I felt as though I had nothing left to give of myself and wanted to die; I felt so totally abandoned.

Every step forward seemed to get knocked back three over the past forty some years. All I ever wanted in life was to grow old with my husband of many years. Watch our children grow up. Our grandchildren come to the same *white picketed fenced house* where our children grew up for Christmas and other family events. The ideal life we all want, and many of us can only hope to get. I felt as such a failure compared to so many other families where they seemed to have their lives securely all-together and moving forward. What was the purpose? What was I doing wrong? I worked hard. I loved everyone intensely. I gave and gave when I had nothing left to give! There was never any expected return in-kind favor, nor an expected expression of gratitude. Always finding some way to be there for whomever needed help.

So, why did I feel as though I was such a failure? Why did my life seem to be everything less of what I dreamed of having? How did I marry two men that were so needy and abusive towards those they loved? They needed so much nurturing, care, and attention for their addictive needs that I was incapable of grasping that serene white picket fenced-in-yard or that Ward and June Cleaver lifestyle. My kids needed a mother that was not busy spending time and energy trying to hold together a dysfunctional lifestyle and trying to make our lives a Cleaver lifestyle that wasn't meant to happen. Little did I know then; that the men I married were themselves children, incapable of being a team partner for me, or a loving and giving father that knew how to be a father image and allow me to be a mother image.

I thought my only accomplishments in life were that I had two beautiful children of my own and a gorgeous grandson. My relationship with Mike was full of laughter, humor, and love in comparison to my two marriages. Through him I had three wonderful children and their offspring had become as my own grandchildren. Not at all how I envisioned living my dream of the white picket fenced house with five children and grandchildren with my "Ward Cleaver" husband. That's the closest I came to my dream. I had been very blessed with my life over the past twelve years with Mike. It was my cloudy vision for the last five years that was messing with my head and heart. I allowed outside influences to affect my attitude towards our relationship.

It took my journey of this most difficult to diagnose, deadliest, rarest, most impossible to overcome and survive breast virus to wash away the mud in my eyes, and to unclog my heart. To truly learn how to love another one of God's souls and give without being drained dry. During my journey I became more in touch with our creator and universe and developed a desire to share some of my experiences and miracles.

There is a thought out there that breast cancer is a result of allowing too many people to emotionally take from you. Many of those who know me feel that this may have been one of the reasons I had gotten breast cancer. This may have been my life before breast cancer, where I gave and gave without the recipient's awareness or returned appreciation. But then over the past two years, I received so many blessings and miracles from other sources to compensate me for all of the gifting I had done.

Anyway, without realizing, I had answered my own prayers to die. The desire to live wasn't there when I started praying to die. Mind over matter can be a powerful thing. Our own *free will* can be very devastating to our physical well being. I had cheated death three times before the cancer, therefore it should be easy enough to let go and die when the fourth time came around? Guess I chose not to go again? Definitely, God said, "No you don't!" It apparently was not the intention of God to take me Home. Once more, it wasn't my time to die. Once more, I've cheated death. What a bummer! Well, I guess I have to wait at least another thirty-five plus years before I'll get to go back Home!

The "bump in the road" (cancer in my life) of my life had been deconstructed, then reconstructed, and newly paved into a smoother road to travel with a better map. The beauty of the scenery on the road as Jesus and I danced has been awesome and full of many blessings. Although, to many, my life may have appeared too tragically eventful, too unsettled, too undecided and financially impoverished at the time of beginning this book, that you might wonder how can I feel so full of joy, peace, hope, and had been given so many miracles? The *scenery and site-seeing stops* along the roadmap that my dance partner and I had experienced as a result of the cancer, I call blessings, miracles, and a transforming awesome journey with Jesus as my dance partner.

Jesus had become *my best leading man* and *dance partner.* Friends, family and acquaintances have and will come and go in my life as time passes, but it always comes down to Jesus never letting go of my hand. He's holding on tight to always protect me in my dance of life against stumbling, falling, or backing into something I shouldn't. He guides me through the dance steps to take, teaching me new ones along the way, and helping me to avoid stepping on His toes. I know my guide, Jesus, will never let go and will always, always continue to hold me once my soul gives up this body, this temple. He will never give up on me and will always be there holding my hand in this journey of life.

I have totally learned to trust Him in our dance together. I have complete confidence that God will always guide me in everything I do. Sometimes other people may have thought I was crazy, but Jesus has been my best guide ever! There have been times I thought the actions He wanted me to do were crazy. But I trusted Him; kept my faith in Him. I did it, not always knowing why, and He always came through for me. In His infinite sense of humor, He sometimes comes through *at the very last possible moment in time.*

For instance, there was a day in 2009 that my daughter and I were flying to a destination for a business trip, and I had no planned place to stay. Literally, as we were setting our carry-on bags down on the seats in the boarding area of the plane for our flight, a friend of mine that I had not spoken with for several weeks called me on my cellular phone. She stated, "I had a feeling to give you a call to see how things are going?" I told her, "My daughter and I are heading out to Phoenix as we speak. We are setting down our bags in the airport at the very moment that you called! How are you?" My friend then asked, "Do you need a place to stay?" "Actually, I do. I hadn't made reservations for anywhere yet. I thought I would take care of that while we waited at the airport for our flight." There couldn't have been a better hotel than the home of my friend. God bless her!

At those moments, I think He was really testing my trust in Him caring for me and watching my back! After all, if you let God, He will guide your steps in your dance of life. He will hold you safe. Let Him be your dance lead.

Chapter Three

The Beginning of My Reinvention

How did it all change for me?

Dr. Ronald Wagner and Marcia Simler

My transformation all began in December of 2007 when Doris called, a previous client of mine I had not spoken with for about six years. She was in tears and told me she and her husband needed some help with their trust. "No problem," I told her. "I know an attorney that can fix the mess, and I'll call him and ask him to contact you and Carl. Then you three can work out your details to get together from that point." Doris expressed a desire to have me there also when they met with the attorney to which I said I can arrange to be there also.

January 2008, we all met at Carl and Doris' home to complete the paperwork to make the changes to their trust. Looking as an aristocrat; dressed in his professionally pressed white shirt, tie, well-tailored trousers, and leather shoes, the attorney was able to make us all feel as though we were having a social event full of laughter and teasing. Before we knew it, the hour appointment was over, the paperwork signed and witnessed, and soon he was wishing everyone a pleasant good-bye.

I remained to reminisce the old times and new events with Carl and Doris. We shared a pizza, teas for supper, and great enjoyment over our being together again treasuring our friendship of over fifteen years. I was so happy to see them again after more than six years had passed without contact with them that resulted from a no compete contract I had from a company I worked with in the past. We were so ecstatic to once again share each other's lives that we hated to see the day rapidly slip past.

We caught up with each other on our important events that had occurred over the past six years. I asked if they knew of the whereabouts of Dr. Ron Wagner who taught us the acupressure classes in 1993. You see, I had been sensing for about three months prior to Doris calling me that I seriously needed to have Dr. Ron balance my body's energy by working on my meridians. My body was not performing as well as it probably could have; it seemed to be short circuiting. Doris and Carl, as always, were eager to share Dr. Ron's information. They graciously added stories and information of Marcia Simler whom they told me could help me with my nutritional and herbal needs. I safely tucked the paper with Dr. Ron's information into a little pocket in my brief case as well as the business card and pamphlets about Marcia.

Knowing that, due to both being in the Madison area, I would need to set aside a day to make the trip to see both; especially Dr. Ron. I felt I had a lot of catching up to do with him, and that could take hours. My procrastination was setting in along with reality of the distance to travel and things to get done. However, at this point in time, it was more important to me to see Dr. Ron because my body was feeling out of sync.

My thoughts were that because it had been over ten years since I've had my meridians balanced that I was extremely over due to have this done. I sensed a meridian balancing as a stronger need at the time than any other type of attention for my body. One of the most valuable lessons Dr. Ron had taught us, and proved to our class, was that if your meridians are functioning properly, any other conventional medical treatment, complimentary herbal treatment, or complimentary therapies work far greater for your body's benefit than when they are not properly functioning. So, Marcia's information was tucked away for future use as well as Dr. Ron's, but it was my intention to make immediate use of Dr. Ron's.

It was time for me to think of heading for the car and a long drive home from Manitowoc to West Bend. It didn't matter. I had a great time. Rekindled an old friendship and went down memory lane reminiscing of the time when we three were taking the acupressure classes in 1993.

As I left with the information that Carl and Doris gave me about Marcia and Dr. Ron neatly tucked into my briefcase, we gave each other hugs and well wishes. Periodically I came across the information that I had secured in my briefcase, looked at it, and tucked it back in my briefcase again for safe keeping. Not realizing when I would pull it out and look at it, how valuable the meeting I had had with Carl and Doris was, and how the information they passed onto me would be worth more than gold, tucking it away for safe keeping only helped me to forget about it and not give it the needed attention until months later.

As yet, I had no indication of what was to occur in my life. I had only sensed that something was eminent, and I needed Dr. Ron's help in the near future.

By the time I met with Carl and Doris in January, I was working on setting up a little office in Madison in another financial planner's office. My task was to provide a college financial planning service to her clients. Little did I know at the time what the real purpose of setting up an office in Madison with an associate planner would be until months later. When the process of fighting for my life had begun; I felt as though all the work, effort and expense of setting up that office was a waste as it no longer exists for me. As quickly as it was set up, it came to an end with the development of the cancer.

However, I *knew* that I was supposed to make the effort and to go through the process of setting up and organizing an office in Madison. Although it didn't make sense to me at the time to head in that direction, I followed what I believed I was supposed to do. If God had not led me down that path, I probably never would have been interested in getting the help that I did from Marcia and Dr. Ron. Had I not been traveling the one and one-half hour distance between Madison and West Bend twice per day, three to four times a week, I very likely would not have considered making appointments with Dr. Ron or Marcia. I think it would have been a definite possibility that I would have given up on the idea of using the complimentary therapies thinking it would have been too far to travel and would then have only done the usual chemo route. That would have meant I would be dead today, as the doctors predicted, and would not have written *Being Held By God*. Actually, I'm not certain what I would have ended up doing because I chose to follow the life path I did instead. But it is a fairly strong assumption that I might not have worked with Dr. Ron or Marcia if these chains of events had not occurred.

So, I could add the acupressure classes I took with Dr. Ron as an event which led to the others, ultimately to my cure and my new life after cancer!

I believe now that God was guiding me towards Madison to go to them for help. To affect my thoughts and feelings about traveling that distance several times a week to see Dr. Ron. Specially to visit Marcia Simler the three or four times I met with her in Madison. Traveling the distance to get help from Dr. Ron would have taken precedence over any other resource in Madison because we had known each other since 1993, and I had never met or talked with Marcia before the cancer.

My symptoms for the inflammatory breast cancer started in March. I had developed a bruise on the upper left of my right breast. I didn't think anything of it when it showed up, because I thought I might have bruised myself from carrying the boxes and furniture for the Madison office. A few weeks later I noticed it seemed to be a little larger rather than smaller, and I placed the inside of my arm against the bruise and it felt warmer than I thought it should. Periodically, I would place my arm on the bruise, and it seemed to get hotter as the days passed, and it wasn't disappearing normally as a bruise dissipates.

Late April, the inflammation of my skin started. It showed up overnight, literally. It wasn't inflamed when I went to bed but was there in the morning when I went to prepare for my shower. When I saw the inflammation, I started to feel scared. While I was getting ready that morning, I brushed the underside of my arm against my breast and it felt very hot! "Oh, Shit!" That was not a good sign! This either meant that I had breast cancer or a breast infection.!! "Damn!! This is not good!!! This could not have occurred at a worse time in my life!"

For a few days I had kept my attention to whether the inflammation was disappearing, increasing or just not changing at all. I think I allowed about a week to pass before I called my doctor for an appointment. Of course, because of the mention of inflammation on a breast I was rushed in for an immediate appointment. The exam was routine and my doctor prescribed antibiotics for ten days, which is the standard procedure whether it's inflammatory breast cancer or an infection. If the inflammation doesn't improve then a second round of antibiotics is prescribed along with the recommendation for a mammogram, which is what had happened.

Victoria Bullis, a psychic and metaphysical healer.

Victoria had been working with me a long time. She had tried to contact me as early as April. She emailed me a number of times as well as called me more than five times, leaving messages of urgency that I contact her. Here was a world-known personality who attempted to get it touch with me who has a following of entertainers, dignitaries, and other highly professional persons! Why!? I wondered about that, but in my mind, *I was so busy.* Busy, setting up the office, getting things up and running in Madison and Milwaukee as a college financial planner that time slipped by rapidly; or so my avoidance allowed me to think.

I didn't want to take the time to call her back. Honestly, it was the fear of what she might have to tell me. Although Victoria was acting on my behalf with concern and urgency in her voice; I was scared. You see, I was trying to avoid my suspicions, and

Victoria's urgent contacts began to confirm those fears I had begun to have about my breast.

A few days after her first contact of concern, my first doctor appointment was scheduled to determine if I was dealing with an infection or inflammatory breast cancer, which was towards the end of April.

I didn't want to know what her concern and panic was about. Victoria had never called me, ever, to warn me of any danger before! *That is so not her style!* One of her first phone calls to me was a day when she was in a London airport getting ready to fly back to Los Angeles; she left a pleading message for me, "Please, please call me the next day! It's important that you call me right away. You can't reach me anymore today because I'm leaving as I speak for Los Angeles. But you must call me!"

Suddenly, I realized that something was very wrong; that what was happening with my body was probably more than an infection.

Ultimately, I called Victoria. My notes showed that we talked about this on May 27, 2008, two days before my biopsy. I wouldn't call me the *queen of procrastination.* Others in my circle of influence take that crown before I. However, there was some serious procrastination by me that occurred at that time.

One of Victoria's greatest and important lessons to me that day was that people type cast you based on what you tell them, or what they perceive of you when they are in your presence; for example, if that conversation has anything to do with age. So now, when people ask me how old I am I'm extremely cautious about what I tell them. Especially, as you reach your golden years it can be more dangerous to casually disclose your actual age. People who come into your sphere of being, will question and wonder to themselves, or ask you, if you have any of the typical physical disorders associated with that age, again particularly, as you reach the golden years of life. *As you think, speak, and believe; so shall it be! It is done!* Therefore, I prefer to be ageless, without age, in the *now*. If you ask me my age, I'll tell you, "I am the age you think I am for today as there is only today. There is only the *now*." Sometimes I'll add, "Let me explain; if you think I am thirty-five, then that is my 'now age' and everything we believe to be associated with that age applies. If you answer '45', then that is my 'now age' and everything associated with that age applies. We are here today, here now, and therefore ageless." That is how I look younger and better than I ever have, in addition to a few other non-surgical practices of mine and visualization. That is how people are amazed at how fantastic I look having experienced cancer! Of course, eating the right nutrition and supplementation for my body is also an immense factor in how well I'm doing and did.

If your belief system is whatever applies to that age you conceive in your mind about yourself, then everything that applies to that age shall become a part of you. Likewise, whomever you think of in the same manner about their age, and believe will happen about their health, so shall it become. I see it happening to people all the time. As soon as you hear the age of someone being fifty, for example, you're questioning whether or not that person has high blood pressure, diabetes, cancer, prostate and so forth. What you wonder about can put the energy out there and so shall it become.

Remember, as you think, God always knows what you are thinking, therefore he now knows what you desire and request. And you could get what you ask for in your thoughts, whether it's for you or someone else. Just a fleeting thought crossing your mind can become reality. This is what Victoria was having me realize about me. Dr. Ron's deer story in Chapter 6 should help you understand this concept even more. As a result of this lesson from Victoria I was very cautious about how I answered anyone's question about the cancer, as well as very guarded with how I told people about it. I always, always, talked about the disorder in the past tense! *Therefore, that dilemma occurred in the past resulting in it not existing in the 'now'.*

Every day take stock in who you are. Such as every day before you go to bed you *intend* to look a little younger when you wake in the morning. Affirmations are *positive* thoughts and prayers; prayers of gratitude to God every moment of your day you are not sleeping. Constant communication throughout the day with God, the universe, the creator, whatever you refer to what I call "God", helps to bring you increasing small and large miracles in your life.

Your constant prayers of *affirmations and gratitude* are more likely to become the *now* if you pray and meditate about them in the past tense; as though they had already occurred. This causes the *future* to more rapidly arrive to you as the *now.* As you work on the emotional, spiritual and mental attitudes of healing, as well as your physical life, don't forget that you need to physically react to what you wish to receive. *Feel the joy and happiness of what it feels like to receive this "gift". Now in the past tense; what did it feel like to have received this "gift".* Also, start acting upon whatever it is you need to do as God's instrument to accomplish receiving this *gift.* In my case, I *knew* that God had a cure for me, and I needed to listen to the messages sent to me to find the solutions to my miraculous cure! I was then the instrument receiving the messages from him and the instrument acting upon them to bring to reality the cure meant for me. Also, through God, numerous key persons brought bits and pieces of my cure to me.

What I learned from golf and a movie called, *The Legend of Bagger Vance*, with Will Smith, was to *keep your eye and intense focus* on the flag (goal, miracle or purpose). Watch this movie several times to further help you grasp this concept. The flag (goal, miracle or purpose) is what you want to have achieved. The flag is the destination you want to get accomplished, *in the past*. As you visualize the flag as though it is right in front of you, that you are there right now, so close to the flag that you can touch it, now hit the ball.

Trust that God and your sub-conscious will work out the details of getting the ball to the flag. Your sub-conscious has already been taught the fundamentals of the game, and God always knows the best possible path to get you where you need to be at any particular time. You just stay focused on the ball already having arrived in the hole at the flag, in the past. What I call the *mechanics of it all* will be worked out as you go.

Victoria instructed me to give thanks to God every night for perfect healing. "I am so grateful that God had healed me. I'm so grateful that I now have perfect health." To the affirmation, or prayer process, I added an activity to my going to bed every night, which I will cover in Chapter Four

Anyway, Victoria discussed in length with me to think no more of aging, because we have been conditioned to believe that as you get older you get sick and you die. Transitions are meant to be good. So it's ok to die and move on to heaven. But, who said that you have to go through all of the illnesses that we are conditioned to go through to get to Heaven when your purpose in life on this planet is complete?

I recently heard of a true story of a young pastor who was at an event. She passed out and was transported to the hospital where they ran numerous tests on her to find out why she passed out. Nothing!! She was sent home in "good health". As the day passed, a friend tried to phone her twice with no response. The friend called for emergency help to meet her at the home of the pastor where they found her dead. The pastor's life's purpose on Earth was complete, and she apparently chose to accept that time given to her to go Home, without having to go through all the debilitating health issues. According to the true story, the autopsy was not conclusive as to the cause of her death. She literally just stopped living! That's for me! I certainly am going to continue making this effort. How about you?

Victoria also worked with me to grow out of the state of hopelessness. She told me that, "If you are in despair and stuck where you are, you still keep hoping and praying for help, and you keep hoping you'll get what you pray for. The issue is that you're not listening to when God wants you to do something else."

As a result of those lessons that day, I practiced the art of communicating daily, by the minute, with God, through my personal guide, Jesus, what he wants me to do with every moment of my life. What he wants me to say every moment of my life. Each day when I get up I ask God to guide me with everything he wants me to do and say for the day. It helps for me to do this, to get through the day, and I know it will help you have a better life.

This had been my key lesson that I'm still experiencing to this day!! This lesson had caused my journey of stage four inflammatory breast cancer that had metastasized to my liver to be a most fantastic ride to this date, and my dance lessons with God have been getting easier and easier.

Thank you, Victoria, for helping me stay on the path God had prepared for me. Thank you, Jesus, for bringing Victoria and I together in 2004 when I heard Victoria on a radio program in Milwaukee.

Chapter Four

God and Faith

A Way of Life

About the time in the process of my transformation and reinvention, I remembered when my daughter was going through her two years of being in and out of the hospital that I had played some cassette tapes with an Irish priest and a woman who prayed and sang the complete rosary. As I prepared for bed, I used to turn on the recorder/player with the cassette tape playing the music and rosary prayers. Once tucked safely in bed I would be tuned into these beautiful Irish melodic prayers of the rosary, knowing that so many miracles had been granted to people who prayed the rosary, that I felt it would only be a benefit playing the musical rosary.

Snuggled under my covers in bed, and as I listened to the musical, I would ask Jesus to come and hold me gently and securely in his arms until I would fall asleep. As I asked Jesus to do this, I would feel an overwhelming sense of peace, safety and assurance that everything would be alright. My body would completely relax as I laid there waiting to fall asleep. Having done that, there seldom was enough time to thank Him for a good day and pray for whatever needed praying as it never took long for my eyelids to seal in a sound sleep until morning.

During those years, many people asked me how was I able to survive getting through those years when my daughter was in the hospital. Having done that process each and every night was my life preserver, my sanity, my soul and spirit's comfort. As I listened to the tunes of the acoustical guitar strings, and the Irish priest and woman as they sang during the prayers helped me to pray. It helped me to feel as though I wasn't praying alone, yet I knew that I was in bed by myself and alone in struggling to save my daughter's life. My parents and grandparents had all passed away nearly ten years before. My husband (now ex-husband) worked third shift and was dealing with his own demons that he is still battling as I write this book.

When my reinvention began, I tried to find where I had packed away the cassettes for safe keeping. However, since I couldn't immediately find where the cassettes were stored, I had to change the process. I had to substitute what I did for something close to what I did when my daughter was in the hospital. I knew where I had the rosaries that were once my mother's and her mother's. One of those first nights during the beginning of my tests; I got one of the rosaries out. After being safely and snuggly tucked in bed I would wrap the rosary around one of my hands, holding the cross in my fingers or in the palm of my hand, I'd kiss the cross and with feelings (sometimes to the point of having tears in my eyes) I'd tell Jesus;

"I love you sweet Jesus. I'm so grateful that you had died on the cross for us, for our sins, and regret that you had to do that for us. Thank you for saving us. Thank you for being my best friend, my business partner, my confidant, and ……..". At this moment I would ask God, and Jesus, to help whomever else needed God's help. Then finally, and again, same as when my daughter was in the hospital, I would ask Jesus to hold me in his strong loving arms until I would fall asleep. I'd ask Jesus, using words such as these, "Jesus, I know you're really busy, but if you could just take a few minutes to come and hold me until I fell asleep, I would love that," or "Jesus, can you come and hold me until I fall asleep?" As quickly as I would whisper these words, I would be sound asleep. There was such indescribable comfort and safety that I felt as I would ask Jesus to hold me. My body could feel His presence with his arms around me as He held me until my body, along with my thoughts, would melt and soften down into deep sleep until morning

When I would awake, my rosary was the first thing I would look for so that I could kiss the cross and thank Jesus for a safe night of sound sleep. Sometimes the rosary was still wrapped around my hand the same as I had done when I went to bed. As the days passed, I began to add asking God to guide me in everything that I did, and to guide me in everything I said. I told Him I was His instrument on earth to do His will. The moment I started this security blanket of using my rosary, I made certain that every night and morning I expressed whatever I was grateful for to Jesus; was the moment I understood that God had plans for me in this lifetime. Regardless of what the doctors were saying about my zero percent survival, I knew God wanted me around for approximately another thirty years. That *moment* with God only confirmed what Victoria told me that I would find the remedy to heal my body and live another minimum of thirty years. This remedy is within *Being Held By God.*

Finally I had found where I had stored my cassettes of the rosary musical. Every recorder player required CD's instead of cassette tapes causing the cassettes to be packed away. I'm sure you can imagine my interest in getting a CD made of these cassettes when Mike had bought a system that allowed him to play the cassette and record it finally onto a CD. It didn't take him long to produce them on the CD's for me. Of course he got a huge hug and kisses for recording the tapes onto CD's for me so quickly. That night I played the disc in my portable player with earphones and continued to play the disc many times in addition to holding my rosary when I went to bed.

One Friday evening in January 2010, I had an intense feeling that it was important that I return to a group meeting that I used to frequent until eleven years before. I struggled with why I needed to go to that meeting. I felt it was ridiculous and a waste of time. But I knew from experience that the *feeling* I had was God telling me that it was important to go, so I went.

The evening turned out to be one of those miraculous moments in time; one of those moments when a messenger, or angel, is brought before you. The energy of that night was at an all-time high level!

After the speaker for the night finished her presentation and the meeting was wrapping up, one of the members recognized me and asked me for an update of the past several years. I told a short version of my story; stated that I overcame stage four cancer in less than three weeks, had explained a little about how I did that, and that I was in the process of writing a book about my journey.

Of course, others heard what I told him. They started to gather around or turn around in their seats. At one point I looked up from writing information down for some of the people that had gathered around where I sat in the last row; I was caught with amazement at the scene of every person in the meeting had turned completely around to face me. Some were standing and others were sitting, but all of them were gathered tightly to me hoping to talk with me, hear me or get information. All were captivated with what I was saying. For a brief snap in time, I felt how it might have been for Jesus when He stood in front of numbers of listeners while He instructed them. For a split second I felt as though I actually stood on one of Jesus' spots where He stood reaching with His (my) arms outstretched. The sensation caught me, made me slightly gasp, at the sight and feeling.

One of the women, Rose Mary, who also had asked for information that night, went to the restaurant that many of the members would go to after the meeting. Rose Mary, as well as some of the members had asked if I would go also. At first, I said, "I think I'm going to head back home." But as more pressured me to go to the restaurant I thought and said, "Well maybe I'll go for a short while." I was the last to arrive there.

Remember, I didn't feel as though I wanted to go to the restaurant, but as I began my drive out of the parking lot I was compelled to drive in the direction of the restaurant. As I walked in, I noticed an empty chair next to Rose Mary, sat down next to her because there was something compelling about Rose Mary that drew me towards her. Apparently, there was a need to spend some time with her that night.

Rose Mary and I were completely captured in the conversation between ourselves that we both ignored the rest of the group. She was going through some rough spots in her life, and we shared with each other some of our life experiences, and at one point I realized that I needed to describe how I would go to bed holding the rosary and listen to the rosary musical prayers.

I described how I would ask Jesus to come and hold me until I would fall asleep. How I knew that Jesus was busy with so many people to look after, but I would still ask Him, regardless of that feeling, if He could just take a few minutes to spend a little time with me, to come and hold me, to come and make me warm if it was a cold night, to love me with His protective arms, to keep me safe as I slept and shield me from the world. Rose Mary was sobbing with joy and a release of restrained emotional pain as I shared this practice with her.

The point is, Rose Mary and I were destined to meet that night. I was to be there that Friday to reach out to Rose Mary to refresh her spirit by elevating her love for God and remind her that God always takes care of His sheep. God always keeps His promises and that everything is in His timing. When He has made whatever we need or desire perfect for us to have we will have what we desire. God placed the desire in you first of all. So, when everything God is working on for you is perfect the desire will occur so quickly and effortlessly, you will feel as though your head spun and you were a marionette.

Rose Mary was meant to help me to realize the title of my book would be called *Being Held By God*. A few other friends and I had been trying to decide on a title for quite some time. My thoughts were that all the titles for a book about a cancer journey had been used. The same for the cover design. The vision of what was to be the cover design also came that same weekend, within twelve hours of each other! Rose Mary ignited a rapid movement in the process of the book as well as a more solid theme. We were meant to meet that night. We were destined to commune with one another that night under God's guidance to help each other move forward with and from the current trials we were experiencing.

As I returned to where I was visiting that weekend, I noticed that an Arizonian friend, Penny, had left me a voice message on my cellular, "Hey, Nann. I just had a vision seeing you before a large crowd in Jesus' robes, preaching!! What was that all about!?" I called her back and left a message on her mobile phone which said, "I know exactly what it means. I had my own similar experience and vision tonight. I'll call you in the morning to explain!"

The next morning, Saturday, I spoke with Penny about our visions. I recapped the event that had happened to me at the meeting the previous Friday night. Penny was excited, and we both agreed that her vision along with my experience and vision was definitely confirmation of what was to come for me. I explained how the event helped me to know the title of my book was to be *Being Held By God* when published. She understood right away, without very much explanation, the meaning behind the title *Being Held By God*.

That same Saturday morning, I spoke with Jan, who helped me get started in becoming an author. Jan is in the process of organizing a publishing business, which made her a great resource.

I excitedly shared with Jan what occurred the night before at the Friday night meeting, with Rose Mary, and with Penny. How I decided on *Being Held By God* for a title. She thought the title would be perfect.

As our conversation progressed, it occurred to me exactly what the cover needed to contain. The cover on this book is exactly as it was meant. As I explained to Jan the cover design, she wasn't sure whether or not there was a connection between the title and the cover. I said, "It has everything to do with the title! It's all about letting God guide you as you would allow your dance partner to guide you during your dance steps.

The one leading you is responsible for your safety, to keep you from falling over backwards, or stepping on someone's foot, keep you from backing into a wall or someone else that is dancing. It's your dance partner's duty to *guide you in every step you take* on the dance floor, or the path of your mission in life." Jan understood what I was telling her, but she was still a little skeptical about matching the title with the description of what I thought should be on the cover.

The following Friday, Jan received an email from her sister, also a writer. Friday was Jan's sister's birthday and her sister wrote a beautiful verse about birthdays and had decided to attach a poem called "Dancing With God" whose author is considered *unknown* as well as written by Elaine L Guercio. I couldn't find proof that Elaine Guercio had written the poem, but I will give her credit for such a beautiful poem which happened to convey so eloquently what I stumbled at explaining to Jan, so here it is below:

"When I meditated on the word **Guidance**,
I kept seeing 'dance' at the end of the word.
I remember reading that doing God's will is a lot like dancing.

When two people try to lead, nothing feels right.
The movement doesn't flow with the music,

and everything is quite uncomfortable and jerky.
When one person realizes that, and lets the other lead,
both bodies begin to flow with the music.
One gives gentle cues, perhaps with a nudge to the back
or by pressing lightly in one direction or another.
It's as if two become one body, moving beautifully.
The dance takes surrender, willingness,
and attentiveness from one person
and gentle guidance and skill from the other.

    My eyes drew back to the word **Guidance**.
When I saw 'G': I thought of God, followed by 'u' and 'i'.
'God, 'u' and 'i' dance.'
God, you, and I dance.
As I lowered my head, I became willing to trust
that I would get **guidance** about my life.

    Once again, I became willing to let God lead.
My prayer for you today is that God's blessings
and mercies are upon you on this day and every day.
May you abide in God, as God abides in you.
Dance together with God, trusting God to lead
and to guide you through each season of your life.
    And I hope you Dance!"

Jan called me about how bizarre it was that she had received this poem from her sister less than a week after Jan and I had talked about the same thing! I told her this type of event was perfectly normal for me; these *coincidental* events occur to me all the time. Jan and I accepted her receipt of Elaine Guercio's poem in such a timely manner as confirmation to us that my title was to be *Being Held By God* and that the cover was to be as you now see it.

Everything in our lives is about our personal relationship with God, Jesus, the universe, the Divine; whatever you want to call the Intelligent Designer. Keep God in your life moment to moment, always close to you, always ask God what to say and do each moment of your day. He will only do what is best for you and those you touch. We just need to listen more to what He tells us to keep us on our life paths. The purpose of our mission in life is the cause of our births, and same will cause our births into the hereafter. To observe what God wants for us is sometimes found in the smallest unrealized event or conversation with someone.

Dance With Jesus!

Chapter Five

Branded – Marked

Emotions When Diagnosed
With a Major Disease.

Late April, my appointment with my primary doctor occurred. After he examined me, he put me on antibiotics to treat me for a breast infection. The antibiotics had begun to run out, and there was no improvement in the inflammation. I called my doctor to extend the prescription for the antibiotics for another ten days, and he required that I have a mammogram done right away. This was and still is standard procedure when someone approaches a doctor with an inflamed breast, as I mentioned in Chapter Three. The idea that I needed to have my antibiotics refilled and that there was no improvement with my breast's appearance began to concern me more than previously.

It scared me to have to see my doctor for my inflamed breast in the first place. I was already somewhat aware of the process that doctors go through before they decide to call it inflammatory breast cancer. Because of my fear of the diagnosis I procrastinated a little with the process hoping maybe it would just go away. No such luck! By now a lump or a swelling had started to make itself known in the area of the bruise.

May19, 2008, Monday, early afternoon, my mammogram was performed.

Hate those things. I hate being squeezed in the manner a woman has to be by one of those machines for a mammogram! As quickly as I had dressed and stepped out of the Radiology Dept. into the waiting lobby of the clinic, one of the lab techs hurriedly approached me to hand me a huge and threatening looking white envelope which contained the filmstrips of my mammogram pictures they had just taken. It still amazes me how rapidly the Radiology Dept had included any previous mammogram pictures I had on file in that envelope! Felt as though it were by magic!

They were rushed and panicky which made me feel panicked. Frightened and worried as to what they saw on the filmstrips; I wondered what was to happen to me next. They tried to be discrete and quiet, but I saw that their behavior was noticed by the receptionist and by the other patients sitting in the waiting lobby. I was standing near the elevator close to the door leading into the Radiology Dept. and reception desk when I was handed the ominous looking white envelope. The nurse told me that I needed to "take the envelope up to see the doctor right away!! He is waiting for you in his office and expects you within the half hour. He is making all his other patients wait so he could see you!" I asked in astonishment, "What do you mean?" The nurse replied firmly and with compassion, "You're supposed to take your mammogram pictures along with you because your doctor is waiting to see you right now to talk with you about them! You have to leave now; he's expecting you in the next few minutes."

My knees became weak with fear! As I looked away from the nurse that was telling me to rush over to my doctor, I noticed that everyone in the lobby was watching us. I felt as though they already knew what that white envelope meant; that the information that it contained was not good and was alarming. They knew what I didn't; that it had to have meant cancer because that was why I was there. Wasn't that so? I began to feel as though I had been marked. Felt that the advertising had been sent out to everyone in the city that Nannette was contagious with cancer and was about to die.

I felt as though I was branded with the word of *cancer* stenciled in red ink on my forehead, as well as any other visible part of my body.

Thank God Mike was on his way to pick me up at the clinic. I had called him before I got dressed to let him know that I was finished at the clinic with my mammogram and ready to leave. Mike had dropped me off for my appointment, so we made arrangements for him to come for me when I called him, and we would then head to the food market. If I had driven there myself, I don't know how I would have handled that event. I just don't know. I'm so grateful Mike was there for me.

He arrived in the waiting room just as I was being told to take my x-rays to my doctor. He is my Rock of Gibraltar. He always makes me feel secure and safe. I remember as we walked out of the clinic, my hand in his, to get to the car, that we both felt shocked.   We felt afraid of what the doctor had to tell me along with concerned about the impact the news hidden in the white envelope would have on Mike's and my life. Was I going to die? Was it a simple remedy, and would we move on with our lives? Very little was said as we drove over to the clinic where my doctor worked that day. We hardly spoke as we drove from the one clinic to another. The fear and concern kept us quiet with our inner thoughts.

It was about 3:00 PM when we walked into my doctor's clinic. We didn't have the opportunity to sit down in the waiting area; I was rushed into my doctor's exam area as quickly as we walked in the door, and through the waiting area. Mike chose to wait in the waiting room. My recent branding was now further reinforced by being rushed through the clinic and to my doctor. I think Mike was afraid to come in to hear what my doctor was about to tell me and wouldn't have known how to handle the news. The staff continued to rush me into one of my doctor's exam rooms where he was waiting for me in his chair! That was a change; not to have to wait for the doctor! As I walked in, saw him literally waiting for me; my thought was that it must be really serious! Many of the usual formalities were eliminated.

My doctor got right to the point. I don't remember whether I sat down or not, or if he gave me another exam or not. I want to believe that he did not examine me again that day, because I only remember my doctor sitting at the desk while I stood in the room inside the doorway as he told me, "You have breast cancer and we need to do a mastectomy right away, within the next few days! It's serious enough that there can be no waiting because it's developing rapidly. I'm scheduling an appointment, as we speak with a surgeon to get things started. The surgery needs to be completed within the next few days!"

Nothing was said about the cancer being at any particular stage at that time. In fact, very little was otherwise said. I was in and out of there in less than thirty minutes.

In the period of those minutes, my fate for the next few months was decided. My doctor wanted me to meet with the surgeon the next day for an exam. Expect to have major surgery within days of the exam I had with the surgeon, have about two weeks of recovery, and think about getting back to work again. OK. I can deal with that. I handled it. Give me the solution and process to get through the event that had been put before me and I'll get it taken care of and move on! Just as anything else that had occurred in my life in the past.

I'm not sure what emotional state I was in at that point. Other than feeling branded, I may have felt some shock to all of that news. Although I don't remember feeling shocked to any great extent. I remember feeling surprised at the news from my doctor. Yet, I wasn't. I think the feeling of shock was well covered when I was handed the x-rays for the mammogram, along with the lab tech's urgent behavior to rush me off to see my doctor when she handed me my film strips. So I was likely in shock by the time I saw my doctor.

My survival and business mode kicked in after the "branding". I was on a mission to come up with a remedy. I knew God was not about to take me home. It just was not the timing for that. So what was the cancer event all about??? It ruined everything, or definitely put a huge detour in our lives!

It was as though traveling along the road you had mapped out for yourself, and now a huge sink hole appears in the road, or a major construction project occurs that no one knew about on your trip plans. But there it was! How should I move forward? What do I have to do to fix that problem? How could I get around it, or pass through it?

I felt as though Jesus threw an extra step into the dance. He caused a huge bump in the road of my life. A few days after the doctor's appointment I asked Him in anger and puzzlement, "What was this all about? What was the purpose of You (God) having this happen in my life; in Mike's and mine? Was this event something that the dark side was using to stop me from doing what I believe You want of me, or was it something You put in front of me to turn the lemons into lemonade for me and others? I am confused!!"

Well, I walked out of the doctor's office into the lobby and collected Mike, who had a worried look on his face. I felt again the looks and stares of the other patients in the waiting area. I knew that they didn't know why their appointment with the doctor got bumped for me, but the feeling of being branded with *cancer* all over me had increased. Mike and I started to talk a little about my meeting with the doctor but had decided to wait until we got in the car. I think he had sensed that I was feeling uneasy about talking about the meeting while in the clinic's lobby.

From that point on, I had decided I was going to do everything possible to avoid looking as though I had cancer. I had decided to refuse to wear the scarf, the bandana, a hat, or any commonly worn trinket or item in public, or at home, that would then announce to the world, "Oh, look at me! I have cancer!" "Oh, No! This is not going to be me! I refuse to give this virus power to kill me! This is not going to be how I'm going to look!"

This is an affirmation I used and still use today: "I am perfectly healthy, and I look perfectly healthy! So be it!"

When you state positive affirmations or positively stated prayers, it is wise to back it up with your activity. As I was just stating above, with that *I AM* affirmation/prayer, I felt I needed to look the part, right?

So, I always wore my wig from the moment I left the bed in the morning until I went to bed, and only removed the wig after the lights were turned out. Every time I went to the clinic I wore makeup and dressed well for the day. Never did I go anywhere with the turban, scarf and *pajama* look. Never did I purchase the cancer turban, hat or scarf. Neither did I receive one that needed to be recycled towards me, or as a gift. I refused to give this virus any kind of power over my life. I think I was quite successful in shaking off the *branded* look, and the feeling of being put in the category of this major illness.

Chapter Six

Two More Messengers From God

Katherine

During May I met with one of my clients, Katherine, with whom I had some discussions about her experiences with her breast cancer. Turned out she started working with Marcia Simler when she was recovering from her breast cancer surgery. She told me when she was diagnosed with her cancer six years before she was scared into having a mastectomy.

She lamented that she wished she had not panicked from the urgent recommendations of her doctors into having the surgery. She wishes now that she had only worked with Marcia back then.

Katherine told me of Marcia's numerous successes with other people who had serious illnesses being freed of the illnesses and diseases. She couldn't recommend Marcia enough. That was the *second time* that Marcia was referred to me. However, I had not yet put together that the person that Katherine, Carl and Doris had recommended to me were one and the same!

An interesting piece of information that I learned later about Katherine's and my relationship was that she was once before put into my circle of angels when my children were small. I needed goat's milk and other organic means of taking care of my children when we were then experiencing health problems from food allergies during the 1980's! Interesting how life works out and life paths keep crossing.

Dr. Ron Wagner

I was so grateful Carl and Doris shared Dr. Ron's phone number and address earlier in the year. It was exactly where I had put it for safe keeping, back in January, knowing and sensing that I would need it soon. I still hadn't made the realization as to how valuable Marcia's information was going to be to me, but I *knew* that I needed to protect it. It was the end of May when I finally took out Dr. Ron's information from that special pocket in my briefcase and called him to make an appointment. Marcia's info was returned to the same pocket in my briefcase for safe keeping.

As I mentioned before, I had been sensing that I needed to have my meridians balanced through acupressure by Dr. Ron. That meant driving nearly two hours from West Bend to Madison and traveling the same back again. At first, I went every three days, then as often as I could throughout August and September of 2008.

Dr. Ron and I had noticed the growth of the tumor in my breast slowing down towards mid-July. It had become less hard and massive. Anyway, in June, Dr. Ron had also told me about how Marcia had helped numerous people overcome cancer and multiple other major health issues. I took her business card from Dr. Ron and tucked it away in my brief case thinking I'd give her a call sometime; maybe in a month or so.

Honestly, I pushed off calling Marcia because I started my appointments with Dr. Ron. My trip to Madison then consumed the day for me. If any friend or family traveling with me had an appointment with Dr. Ron, it would then be a very long day; early morning through to late at night before we would arrive home. We could travel three to four hours to make the trip, and many times we'd stop for a meal at a restaurant in Madison before heading back to West Bend. So to add another forty-five-minute drive further west was daunting for us. A visit to one of Marcia's closest clinics would have made the drive time for the day nearly six hours. After spending almost four hours visiting with Dr. Ron, all we could think about after we were done was to get a meal and head for home. At the time, those thoughts and feelings were causing me to not find the value of getting involved with Marcia. Everything caused me to feel overwhelmed.

That was the *third time* that Jesus has guided me to take a step in our dance to work with Marcia and make use of her skills for my cure. Frequently, during my trips, Dr. Ron kept reminding me to call Marcia. Had I connected the dots of the information about Marcia from Dr. Ron with that from Katherine, Doris and Carl, that their referrals were all about the same woman, I think I would have responded immediately to God telling me what to do. But "no", I had to be "hit over the head" one more time. A fourth alert or message referring Marcia had to occur for the light bulb to have gone on. The epiphany from God that He wanted me to work with Marcia hadn't occurred. I didn't hear the messages; didn't realize that I had received messages from three different sources for the same woman!! Whereas, the *knowing* that I had to work with Dr. Ron was a little more subtle. Figure that out!

Sometimes we are too blind or deaf to realize what God is trying to help us with, and we reject it. Or we allow our feelings or pride to cloud the directive or message. Just as the story of a man who was drowning, and he was praying to God to rescue him. God sent him two rescue boats to save his life, but the man refused their aid, so they continued forward leaving this man to drown in the water. Finally, the man drowned, went to meet God, and the man had angrily questioned God why He hadn't answered his prayers for God to save him! God said He did send two coast guards to take him to shore, but he refused the help! God had tried to help the man in answer to his prayers, but the man was blind and deaf to how God would send the help. *Me Too*! God always answers His promises to you, so we need to not be blind and deaf to how He will do it.

He is always watching our back. Let Him do it. Sometimes more subtly than others, and sometimes it seems like a blunt blow to the head. We do have free will to accept His aid, or not.

Dr. Ron learned his skills in the Orient as a young man, and I have known him since 1993 when I studied acupressure with him. This was the class where I had met Doris and Carl which was an illuminating experience.

With Dr. Ron I was able to get a number of things realigned, adjusted, and prayed over to make my body healthy. He taught me how to think of the cancer as a virus and congestion that needed clearing.

Actually, if you do some research into any of the medical files on the internet you can find numerous documents calling cancer a *VIRUS!!!!* That information helped me to refocus my thought processes with what was going wrong in my body.

I started to seriously focus on finding out what I had to do to fix whatever was going wrong with my body and less on the current symptoms. This is an important thought and realization. Focus on how to fix what is going wrong. What is the source? Not cut away (remove) the symptom. Not drug away the symptom. The time had come to fight for my life and definitely believe the doctors' diagnosis of zero percent survival was wrong.

I *knew* that God had plans for me with my life, and I had to find the way He wanted me to fix what did not work right in my body. What was it that needed to be done? Get it done. Fix the source of the *bump in the road* and get the bump in the road resolved and move forward.

From Dr. Ron I already knew not to give this virus power by giving it current authority over me from Dr. Ron. Not to give it a *present tense* in any of the words I used about the disease. I always referred to this event in a *past tense* as though it was something that had occurred to me in my past. *Never* did I use the statements of, *"I am* diagnosed with cancer", or *"I have* cancer". I always made the verbal statements of *"I was* diagnosed with stage four inflammatory breast cancer *that had* spread to my liver and surrounding lymph nodes." *Whatever you verbalize in the present and past tense, you give power and energy to, and whatever you think in the present and past tense, so shall it be. Our bibles tell us this, also.*

Words have a lot of power; be careful how you use them. Thinking and verbalizing positively is always more beneficial to you and your world, than the use of negative thoughts and negative words.

As I saw Dr. Ron again, I remembered some research I had done years before where I had learned about curses and blessings. Curses are as negative thoughts, and words of curses are negative energy that gives your curse more power.

Whatever, or whomever you have cursed becomes bestowed with negative energy, and you have just cursed the very same to yourself as well; for four generations! The same happens when you bless events, things or persons. These are positive affirmations of thought and positive verbal blessings which likewise add to the strength of the blessing, and last four generations also.

For instance, while you are angry with someone you blurt out that you wish that person would be condemned to the opposite place of Heaven. I'm not going to specifically use the words, because I only wish everyone to go to Heaven. I'd rather bestow you with positive energy and blessings, so therefore, "I wish you would go to heaven!" There, that will last you and your lineage for four generations. Now, how that is accomplished will be between you and God.

How the use of grammatical negative words impacts your well being, please read the following story that Dr. Ron gave me. I believe it will help you with creating a positive thought instead of a negative thought; a blessing rather than a curse.

The Parable, if you will: you're driving along a road through a forest where you know that deer could likely roam. So your fear is to avoid hitting a deer with your car, right? Rather than thinking and talking about being a afraid of hitting a deer that crosses the road you are traveling on; where would you rather see that deer? Or, where should that deer be other than crossing your path? Three of the answers to his story were: one, either sleeping all warm and comfy in their den in the woods miles away from you and the road. Or, two, if you want to see their beauty and grace then see them a mile away running in the opposite direction. Then, thirdly, gracefully eating in the field at a distance without a care about you being on the road in your car! *Then that is what will happen! As you think, so shall it be! As you speak, so shall it be! As you visualize, meditate, and pray, so shall it be! But be cautious of what you ask for!!*

Therefore, your best positive thoughts and verbalization would be of the deer sound asleep, nice and warm, tucked away in their dens miles away from where you are on the road safe and secure, and you are left safe and secure enjoying your drive. Your belief must be absolute with this. There cannot be the least amount of doubt or question within your being.

Matthew 21:22, "If you believe, you will receive whatever you ask for in prayer." *James 1:6-8*, "But when he asks, he must believe and not doubt, because he who doubts is like a wave of the sea, blown and tossed by the wind. That man should not think he will receive anything from the Lord; he is a double-minded man, unstable in all he does."

Again, thinking or saying, "I hope I don't hit a deer!" is the negative grammatical version. The word "don't" is the negative word which your subconscious is not able to understand. Your conscious mind has to convert it to an immediate comprehensive thought or statement. Take "don't" out of the sentence or thought, your sentence or thought now becomes "I hope I hit a deer!" That now becomes an affirmation, your prayer, or your desire, because your subconscious only recognizes positive types of words, absolute types of words, and will work on creating this for you without any additional conscious effort on your part.

This thought process and verbalization was far more soothing to me and relaxing, than getting nervous and worried about hitting the deer crossing the road I was traveling! So I started focusing more and more on thinking and talking that way. I didn't want to bring negativity, stress, and uneasiness to my lifestyle more than I could help it, so I paid more attention to where I was visualizing the location of the deer, if you will.

Same as whenever the word *deer* enters in your mind while you're driving; every time the word *cancer* would enter my mind, or the seriousness of it, I would immediately change my thoughts to God sending down His healing energy into me. It would travel throughout my body from head to toe to wherever there might be cancer virus cells. The energy flowing through my body would separate into laser beam types of healing energy that would seek out these cells and zap (vaporize) the tiniest molecule of this virus into nothingness. **POOF! Gone!**

I know this worked for me because while I still had the cancer this technique was very easy to *feel* and *see* in my mind that the cancer cells were being vaporized by the laser beams; whereas now that the cancer is gone, this event doesn't occur. It's as though the switch is flipped off now as soon as the energy would flow into my body. Now, whenever I attempt this technique there's an abrupt stop to the *laser beams*, preventing them from radiating outward towards those viruses I once had. Or, I see it just flowing in and immediately dissipating without seeing the *laser beams* destroying the nasty cells.

Those techniques were my *deer sleeping in its den*. Had Dr. Ron not given me this visual, this parable or story, I very likely would have continued thinking of my breast as being sick, as ill, or as diseased. I started reprogramming my thinking to less of the *deer hitting the car* scenario, and more to where the *deer are sleeping safely in their dens.*

He also taught me how to visualize my breast in its once healthiest form and condition. He gave me an illustration of what the interior of a healthy breast would look like without the congestions (tumors). He taught me the purposes of the lymph nodes surrounding my breasts which are there to help cleanse the toxins out of the body. He instructed me in massaging my arm from my hand along my arm towards my chest as I showered to free up the clog in the lymph nodes, similar to clearing a jammed drain under your sink.

Sorry about that drain visual.

Chapter Seven

Graviola – Cancer Cure

Melvin Simonovich

Here is another one of Jesus' messages and messengers to me. As I was telling Mel about my diagnosis, he told me about a newsletter that he recently received from a health institute discussing the benefits of graviola. That the graviola is reported to be 10,000 times more effective than chemotherapy! He wasn't aware of where to get the herb. He did, however, email the newsletter to me to take a look at what it had to say.

Mel was very excited about an herb he was using which he learned about through the same institute for a medical concern of his own. He said he was having amazing results for himself and was quite adamant of the likelihood of the graviola helping me, because anything that he had researched as a response to the newsletters he received from the health institute and used for his own medical needs were successful. Regardless, I had nothing to lose. It became my total focus to find out more about that graviola stuff, find it, and get it. It sounded fantastic to me!

Hopefully, it would be a definite solution.

I had a purpose, a prompt from God to find out more about this *graviola* and get my resources for the herb. Again, what could I lose?

My other option was far more gloomy and deadly! It was my intent to find a solution to my dilemma. I decided that at that point in the process either the graviola would be the only possible remedy, or as an addition to any other I had yet to decide upon. Learning about the graviola gave me more hope.

Things started to occur and became promising. The *reconstruction of the bump in the road* had progressed. The future was yet to unfold, this was only the beginning.

Mel suggested searching the internet to track down how to get the graviola. The same day we talked; I received his email from HSI (Health Sciences Institute) to get me started. My full-time job became researching anything I could find through the internet using the information contained in the email that Mel had received from the HSI.

After diligently searching the internet for several weeks I finally found Raintree Nutrition out of Las Vegas. I was impressed at what I saw on their website. They had amazing testimonials, a list of practitioners that use their products throughout the country, along with suggested usage for yourself and your pets!

As I dug deeper into the graviola and its benefits, I was able to find other clinical research papers and stories about the two graviola trees found in South America.

I decided to use their N-Tense product which contains both of the graviola trees that grow in the South American rain forest along with a few other herbs that are beneficial for someone with cancer. I still use the N-Tense product today in this manner: two capsules in the morning, and two at bedtime for thirty days, then take a break for sixty days, and repeat the dosage for thirty days in that cycle.

I would continue this process until graviola is not available or until the day I go to the hereafter. If you have not had or do not have cancer, then taking the graviola for thirty days every six months could possibly help to prevent cancer.

The Raintree Nutrition website has an article which discusses a major pharmaceutical company that had tested and researched graviola as a cancer cure, that the graviola is 10,000 times more effective than chemotherapy. The article stated also that the pharmaceutical company destroyed over seven years of case histories and research when it couldn't get a patent on the graviola plant. As a result of not getting the patent, because patents are not granted on plants, the major pharmaceutical company could not get FDA approval!!!

I think it's very devastating that the money to be made from a patented medicine was more important to the pharmaceutical company than sharing that they had research to back up the fact that graviola can be a cure for many cancer sufferers!

Agreeably, I believe that any plant that God created, or plant that had evolved from a plant that God created, should never be in a position to be patented by any company for the purpose of profit for that company because the company was willing to *buy* the patent! Gratefully, the company couldn't get the exclusive rights to the plant with the patent, leaving God's intelligently designed plants, which He put out there in the world for us to pick as a whole or original part to use for our bodies' health and well-being without prescription. God's perfectly *designed plant* is useless as man's recreation, which doesn't resemble a cell of the original plant, which may have serious side effects and might kill you or create more side effects than an herb. My other irritation is that this pharmaceutical company would have greatly overcharged for the graviola as a prescription, claimed all types of rights to the cure, and made more wealth on the graviola than you and I can imagine.

Needless to say, I remember being relieved and happy when my first shipment finally arrived on June 17, 2008! Must have more emotionally counted on it arriving than I had anticipated. My medical team was still running tests to determine what was happening to me.

Should they diagnose me with cancer, or something other than cancer?

What stage I should be put under?

Was it inflammatory breast cancer or a more common type of breast cancer?

How were we going to proceed with managing the dilemma? Seemed like a headache to me!

Chapter Eight

First Biopsy

May 22, 2008, Thursday, I went to a clinic in West Bend to meet the surgeon for the first time. His background for over twenty years had been in the particular field we had been discussing. May 22nd turned out to be an eventful day! It was a turning point in the course we seemed to have been heading.

By now I've started to notice a lump in my right breast in the area where the bruise had been for the previous two months. At the time of the biopsy the bruise was nearly gone, and the inflammation was worse and hot, along with an increase in the swelling of my breast.

So I prepared myself with the gown, propped myself on the clinic bed and tried to relax with my eyes closed. I decided to meditate, or dream, of being on a warm beach in Maui as I waited for them to come in and introduce themselves to me and I to them. That day, trying not to get anxious about what was about to occur at the appointment, I made an effort to keep my frame of mind as though it were just another routine checkup.

The usual protocol occurred when a doctor, nurse and patient meet each other for the first time. Dr. Jewett and his nurse, Shelly, were very friendly and compassionate, and I liked them immediately.

Dr. Bryan Jewett started to examine me, and I noticed his face expressed some bewilderment as he made the comment, "Something doesn't seem just right. There is something out of the ordinary when compared to the normal types of breast cancer."

It looked and felt different from the routine type of breast cancer where we could have headed off to surgery the next day for a mastectomy. His expression became that of concern as he stated, "We might be dealing with inflammatory breast cancer. We're going to run some tests before deciding about the mastectomy."

I later learned that there were less than five oncologists in the state of Wisconsin who had any familiarity or experience in working with inflammatory breast cancer. For that matter, the ratio of doctors with this type of experience is just as low anywhere in the country. These doctors were too far away from me to travel to every other day, as well as possibly not in my insurance plan. But I was fine with my team taking the time to research and connect with their network of such doctors to help me with my needs. So I stayed with my medical team.

We all agreed that I should go back on Thursday, May 29, 2008, for the biopsy. Dr. Jewett's expression of puzzlement as to the type of cancer they wanted to diagnose me with started my commitment of wanting the doctors to be absolutely positive of what was going on with my body.

What type of cancer or other disorder so that I'm treated correctly? Right?

Not to be incorrectly diagnosed and treated. I have personally known too many people that had been misdiagnosed, treated wrongly, and because of it, died. Including myself, twenty years prior, for an accident I had.

It was time to start taking matters into my own hands. It was time to start researching breast cancer, especially inflammatory breast cancer. Find out what causes cancer, if I could, and learn the different sides of the story from the medical industry and the alternative complementary therapies.

Next, determine what I have to do to fix the cause of my cancer, and not just the symptoms.

After all, isn't cancer a virus, or as an allergic reaction? Some sort of chemical imbalance in the body, and the response to that could be cancer or some other major disease? I had to be prepared to decide whether I needed to combine the two to repair my body or pick one over the other to heal my body.

May 29, 2008, 1:00 pm, I had my Breast Biopsy with my surgeon, Dr. Jewett, which was an Ultrasound guided right breast core and punch biopsy. I took a taxi over to the clinic Thursday, and Mike picked me up after I was done.

I remember going in with a matter-of-fact attitude, but internally, I was nervous and dreaded finding out what was going on in my breast, yet I was eager to get to the bottom of everything and move on with my life.

After I got dressed for the occasion with one of their stylish gowns, I was led to the room where the biopsy was to be performed. As I was made comfortable and sedated, the ultrasound equipment was brought in along with the biopsy needles for the procedure they performed that day. In my drunken frame of mind Dr. Jewett, his nurse, and I chatted during the procedure, however at one point they needed to show me a biopsy needle that had just bent nearly forty-five degrees!

Apparently, that had never happened before! They were awed that my tumor had become so hard that it bent one of their biopsy needles!

Through my drugged-up awareness I thought the bent needle they showed me was quite impressive! No one thought that my tumor that grew in my breast had developed so much at that point to have bent a biopsy needle!?

June 4, 2008 10:00 AM, I went back to see Dr. Jewett for a follow up on the biopsies. Jewett was pleasant yet subdued. He didn't have good news for me.

At that point, the results of the biopsies showed that it was breast cancer; however the skin biopsy was negative as to inflammatory breast cancer. Although given the inflammation, the orange peel-look of my skin, and the bruise, Dr. Jewett clinically diagnosed me with inflammatory breast cancer. Not always will the biopsies prove positive for inflammatory breast cancer and must be clinically diagnosed by the appearances of the breast.

He told me that based on the May 19 mammogram the size of the tumor then was at least 3-4 cm, and that unfortunately my antibody and receptor results (ER PR receptors) were both negative which made treating the cancer more dangerous and complicated to overcome. At a later appointment Dr. Jewett had told me that my situation was "a life ending event".

That day was a long day. We mulled over my situation at some length. Dr. Jewett answered all of my questions and told me that Dr. Abhay Jella, my oncologist, wanted to see me first before beginning any neoadjuvant treatment. They both felt they needed more tests completed before beginning any treatment.

Dr Jewett said he would be happy to put in the MediPort for me should I agree to go ahead with the neoadjuvant chemotherapy. He also told me he ordered some additional laboratory studies and a CT scan of my chest, abdomen and pelvis. He told me my first appointment with Dr. Jella was scheduled for the following week and that the CAT scan needed to be completed in the next few days before meeting with Dr. Jella. The CT Scan occurred on the same day as my first meeting with Dr. Jella.

Dr. Jewett asked about my support system. Who would be there for me as I went through this, and how was my family taking the news? I told him that I had no family in the area and had informed a few friends but didn't know how they took the news and how they would behave towards the news in the future to be a support system for me.

I had not broadcasted the news to everyone, only a few people were told at that time because I didn't exactly know how my diagnosis would turn out. I stated I had a daughter who lived in the community, but we hadn't talked for quite some time, so I didn't think she would be any type of support or part of a support system for me. She was totally wrapped up in her relationship with her boyfriend. My son lives in California with his family. They've been after me to move out there, or at least spend more time in Orange with them. So their support would be from a distance unless I moved out there. My sister lived five hours away, so I'd have to move there, also. My brother was too hard to get in touch with, and he was going through family issues of his own and wasn't remotely in any position to help me.

During the conversation I couldn't think of anyone from my friends and family that would be a part of my support system other than my true-blue loyal love and sweetheart, Mike. After all, I was going to live forever, why would I have set up a specific support system for this type of thing?!!

Oh, well. I indicated I'd work something out. I liked Dr. Jewett's and Shelly's compassion they showed towards me that day and how they had made every effort to make me feel cared about as well as supported. They gave all the time I emotionally needed without being pushed through the system.

Thank you, guys! You were a blessing when you were brought into my lives back then.

Nevertheless, it was a lengthy visit with the surgeon along with tears, hopelessness and being put in a position of now trying to figure out what next I should do. He strongly recommended getting my family to help me and to consider moving closer to family that would be a support for me.

I stayed with Mike; he was compassionate towards my needs at that time and graciously cared for me and told me not to worry about moving closer to my family.

Chapter Nine

The Diagnosis

More Delays Until God's Time Was Perfect

June 10, 2008, Tuesday, 9:30 am, CT Scan of the chest, pelvic, and abdomen at the Hartford Clinic. They were unable to do the scan completely as they would have liked. The contrast chemicals they wanted to give me had the potential of being iodine based, and because of the family history with iodine sensitivity, the lab technician backed off giving me the contrast. We decided to do the scan anyway with only the barium milkshake in my body and see what would show up.

This slowed the diagnosing process down a little, which turned out to be a good thing because I was a little slow to recognize the messages from my guide, Jesus, to call Marcia Simler of Natural Health Works in Madison. That He wanted me to work with her to create my miracle that God had been working on providing me. I just wasn't connecting those dots, you know. I still hadn't been "hit hard enough over my head" to recognize the rescue ships sent me.

Later in the day, I met with Dr. Jewett at 1:00 PM to go over the results. The initial read by the radiologist stated there was no obvious tumor in the right breast, but that there was an area of increased soft tissue density in the mid and outer right breast that might represent the neoplasm. There were multiple enlarged lymph nodes in the right axilla, and some questionable density in both of my liver lobes. Apparently, the scan showed a 3.3 cm hypodense mass in the mid left lobe of the liver and a 2 cm hypodense mass in the mid right lobe of the liver, but it was otherwise difficult to read because of not using the iodine contrast.

Lab results from the blood drawn on June 4th showed my cancer antigen (BR27-29) had increased from 0-40, which is normal for someone without cancer, to 58.4. My other lab results were normal. Dr. Jewett thought the best approach was to go ahead and schedule a PET CT scan to further decide if these areas in the liver were anything to worry about, which we did. The PET scan would give us a look at any other potentially metabolically active areas in my body, therefore a PET scan seemed to be the right way to go and should be done right away before I met with Dr. Jella, the oncologist.

That same day I had my first meeting with Gloria, the Breast Cancer Coordinator at the clinic; immediately after the CT scan and before I met with Dr. Jewett. Our meeting involved a discussion of my diagnosis of the moderately differentiated invasive carcinoma along with inflammatory breast cancer, and my first appointment with Dr. Jella, the oncologist, was scheduled for June 16th.

Gloria gave me a breast cancer binder, which she used to present to me the different businesses available to get wigs, hair pieces, hats, and turbans. At which I bluntly pointed out to her that I wear a suit every day, and I was not about to wear any of those items other than a wig! She pursued my wearing some of the nice hats that are available because the wig can be hot to wear in the summer heat.

I was determined that I would only wear the wig instead of a cancer advertisement on my head, known as the hat, scarf, bald head or turban regardless of how hot it got outside. I strongly, and with authority, told Gloria that wearing a wig was how I was going to look normal and cancer free, how I was not going to advertise having the cancer and prevent the cancer from having power over me.

If it was hot and humid, desert summer heat, winter storm, go swimming, going to the shower as I first woke up in the morning or right after turning off the light to go to bed, the wig would be and was always worn!

I refused to give the virus power or control over my health.

I refused to give the virus ownership over my body by daily going around advertising that I had been diagnosed with that dreadful thing.

I explained to Gloria that wearing anything other than a wig would be giving in to the disease and giving it power to kill me. Wearing anything, even a bald head, would be advertising to the world while wearing one of those symbols that I had that horrible event occurring in my body and life! Absolutely no way was I going to look any other way than normal at home or especially in public.

That included learning how to make me look good with my makeup once I lost my eyebrows and eyelashes. If I had lost my fingernails, I would have found a way to wear tips on my fingers so that my fingers would look manicured, if not normal.

She also encouraged me to get registered with the "Look Good, Feel Better" program and the ABCD (After Breast Cancer

Diagnosis) program to get a mentor to help me through the cancer journey. She wanted me to be prepared and to know that there were support systems out there because it could get overwhelming with all the doctors' visits. Gloria stated that I could call with any questions or concerns I might have had down the road. I hope I didn't push her away too severely, she was trying to help me, but I only gave the information she gave me partial interest and consideration.

I had a very strong sense that this was not to be the path that this event in my life would take me. The death and gloom path that it felt they were trying to lead me on, was not at all what I believed was to be my journey!

June 16, 2008, 9:40 AM, Monday, the day after Father's Day was my first appointment with my oncologist, Dr. Jella. My tumor had noticeably increased in size since the May 29th biopsy. I suspected that the biopsy had greatly irritated the tumor, because after the biopsy date the tumor seemed to rapidly increase in size, almost daily it seemed.

Dr. Jella's report, from that date, stated an appearance of inflammation, a peau d'orange dimpling of my skin, and the mass overall roughly measured 5 to 6 cm. The mammogram of May 19 showed the mass as 3-4 cm in size. My breast had grown 2 cm in less than a month!! For me that meant loosening my bra to allow for the increase in size and provide for my breast's comfort.

At that appointment the doctors were still uncertain as to whether, or not, the diagnosis was to be inflammatory breast cancer or not, although all clinical appearances were beginning to indicate more and more that inflammatory breast cancer would have to be their decision. Dr. Jella scheduled additional lab work and tests at that appointment such as the PET Scan

June 18, 2008, Wednesday afternoon, went to the Slinger clinic to have the PET Scan performed. After having been poked, stabbed by needles, drank barium milkshakes, injected with contrast and who knows what; bared my breast and torso so many times that I felt I could have made a lot of money as a stripper. June 18 created a new experience to add to my list of lab work and doctor visits!

The end of my patience and tolerance had arrived from all of the tests, lab work, stress, panic, doctor visits, and time off of work because more than one and one-half months had been focused on running around the county for the testing, counseling, and my own personal research as to how to remedy what had rapidly happened to me and everyone around me, as though overnight! I felt as if my whole life exploded in front of me, and everyone I loved and knew was now within its shrapnel.

I went with mixed feelings about having the PET Scan. I was happy that I was scheduled for the test that Wednesday, because it was one more step closer to getting this whole research process over with so we could move forward. It was time to stop randomly running around the county for all the testing that was done. I had been dealing with doctors, clinics and staff for three months since the inflammation showed up!

I'm content and happy that the doctors did everything possible to be absolutely certain of my diagnosis; personally, having known too many people that had been misdiagnosed for cancer and other medical situations. Some of these people were diagnosed with cancer, treated with chemo, died within weeks of the treatment and their families were told that the person never had cancer and the chemo killed the person.

Myself, included, was diagnosed twenty years ago, as a result of an accident that the injury to my hip was only a broken blood vessel and everything would clear up within eight weeks. It didn't. In fact, the injury became worse, and I was later told by another doctor that if I had I fallen on my hip again, I would have ended up in a wheelchair permanently! Consequently, my hip muscle did not correctly heal and causes problems to this day.

I think this was an important attitude that I had. That all the research and test results needed to be completed before any cutting or poisonous dumping of chemicals into my body. I took a proactive approach to what was happening to my body and what was about to happen. I did my research to the best of my ability. Investigated all the possible remedies to what I felt my body and I needed. I felt that I had closely analyzed the events that occurred around me and observed and listened intently for directives from God to do what He wanted me to do. I do believe my attitude helped to drag out the time until God had everything in place for my miraculous healing!

So, needless-to-say, with the seriousness of this medical event I wanted the doctors to be positive; without any doubt, of what we were dealing with! After all, I was looking at poison being pumped into my body to make it healthy again!! Where was the logic in that?

And wasn't this treatment method only treating the symptoms?

So, I was determined to find the cause of what went wrong in my body. There was a cause to this all, and it was important to find the cause and treat or fix the cause, not just the symptom! *When only the symptom is being treated or cut away, will it not come back elsewhere?*

The taxi took me to the clinic for the PET Scan as I was hesitant to drive myself there and Mike picked me up on his way home from work. I had noticed that some of the tests made me sick or drowsy that I felt it was safer to have someone drive me to the clinic and pick me up when I was finished.

The PET Scan radiologist led me through the halls of the hospital to outside to a beautiful summer day and onto a platform attached to a semi-truck. The elevator platform had a metal railing with a gate attached which the fellow closed behind us and picked up a cable with an electrical box holding two buttons. The buttons probably were for "up", and the other for "down".

The elevator raised the lab tech and I up to the door level at the middle of the trailer. Once at floor level, he lifted a huge garage type door up into the cavity of the trailer's roof exposing a room of computers, screens, a desk cluttered neatly with papers and files along the opposite wall of the trailer. The other male radiologist introduced himself as Mark and took me to the right of this space into a little room that contained three large lounge chairs and had me sit down in one.

Mark told me to find a position that I would have to stay in for nearly forty-five minutes to allow the contrast to prepare itself for the PET Scan. So, I took a relaxed position in the reclining chair. After Mark covered me with a warmed blanket and proceeded to attach the I.V. equipment to my arm for the contrast, he then brought out a chilled stainless steel type of drum which contained a radioactive contrast designed to hunt out cancer cells in a body and proceeded to attach it to the I.V. for injection. Mark said, "Don't move or talk for forty-five minutes to prevent the contrast from collecting in an area that it is not supposed to go, such as your throat or the inside of your arm's elbow. So just rest here, quietly, and I'll check on you in a few minutes. OK?" As I waited my turn, I closed my eyes, and meditated on the cancer being gone. That God was sending His healing energy down into my body through my head.

After forty-five minutes of snoozing in my recliner, my turn came for the scan. Mark removed the blankets covering me and led me out of the little room through the room with all the computers and screens, into a much larger room to the left of the control room.

This room had windows in the wall between it and the control room allowing the radiologists to observe the *donut* perform its task. He led me to the table where he had me lie down on it, propped some pillows under my knees and a pillow for my head. He made sure that I was not wearing anything that contained any metal for the scan. He asked if I was comfortable, and once I was, he headed out into the area we had just passed through.

The table moved forward or back as the radiologists positioned my body in the scanner. I thought it was fascinating to get this scan done on my body. I've seen scanners used to scan mummies on the history channel and thought it was extremely interesting to see what was contained inside of the mummy. So, I was excited to see my pictures, and what my body would look like! I had to wait until July 2nd to finally see the pictures of my scanned body which was difficult for me.

Things like this captivate my interest, and I always wonder how they work. What is it that a machine can do that we can't, being made in the image of God? Why do we trust a machine to *see* and *sense* what we think we can't?

June 26, 2008, Thursday, 8:30 AM met with Dr. Jella. He informed me of the results of the PET Scan but didn't have the pictures. I was disappointed that he didn't have the PET scan pictures! It was important to me to see my pictures of my body. He told me I had numerous *hot spots* in my upper right chest that were affecting my breast, upper liver, thyroid, and numerous surrounding lymph nodes.

It was a sad day.

It was a definite *you're going to die day.*

The PET Scan showed numerous axillary lymph nodes with abnormal FDG activity. SUV not reported. My right breast had FDG activity of 22.9 with diffusely thickened skin of the right breast, which confirmed inflammatory breast cancer. The thyroid gland inferior right lobe had SUV 9.2 and the anterior thoracic wall along the internal mammary chain had increased activity of SUV 3.5. There was an ill-defined hypodense hepatic lesion at the dome of the liver, which demonstrated abnormal FDG activity of 17.5.

June 30, 2008, 3:00 PM Wednesday. An MRI of my brain was done that day, and it was my son's 32nd birthday. What a way to celebrate one's son's birthday! Again, the same process to get into the semitrailer with the elevator, to receive the contrast, the only difference was the donut for my head. All they could find was a mild ethmoid sinus mucosal thickening. And, yes, they did find a brain in there! It was not an empty cavity! So, this was a relief that they could find no *hot spots* in my brain. In other words, there was no cancer. That was a sigh of relief!

July 2, 2008, 7:34 AM, Wednesday: West Bend clinic. I met with Dr. Jewett, my surgeon, to discuss a follow-up on the diagnosis and the installation of the MediPort. At last I was able see the pictures from my PET Scan, and in glorious color! I was fascinated and excited to have actually seen what was going on inside my body. It's totally fascinating to me how these work and what they are capable of showing.

Dr. Jewett's nurse, Shelly, was generous in giving me a CD disk of the pictures from the PET Scan and showed me the locations of the hot spots. It was shocking to see how much of my right upper chest was lit up like a heavily lit Christmas tree with bright white lights in total darkness! Dr. Jewett and I also went over the information on the MediPort, how it works, and where he would place it in my shoulder.

He discussed with me how Dr. Crain would do the liver biopsy. There was a lot of concern with the procedure as the hot spot on my liver was right behind my lower right lung. They were concerned about accessing one of the liver's upper lobes without puncturing the lung. If the lung would have been punctured, I and my doctors would have been thrown into an emergency surgery to rescue my lung and life.

Dr. Jewett had a lot of confidence in Dr. Crain, so I wasn't worried either, but I informed my kids and family that I might not have survived the biopsy, or that there could have been an emergency surgery.

We again touched on the conversation about my kids and family and support from them. How the support from my kids had been less than I had expected from them, which was very little. They were young and very much into themselves, and it hurt that they didn't seem to care about their mother more than they had shown. I learned later that my kids, family and many of my friends didn't grasp the severity of my diagnosis until nearly two years later!

Amazing! It must have been my overall positive attitude about life and my outcome that may have caused them to believe the diagnosis wasn't as severe as it could have been and was. It goes back to the "As you think and speak, so shall it be." If everyone else around you have the belief that everything is going to be fine about you, it will. Therefore, it's crucial to have your circle of influence believe you *are* healthy, that the end result will be health instead of sick or poor.

I do like Dr. Jewett. He has a genuine care for his patients and sensitivity. I'm afraid I was the one that was more matter of fact about the processes that happened to me. I just wanted to get through that stage in my life and move forward. I just wanted it all to be over and done with so I could get on with my life, right? Let's get this problem fixed and move on and enjoy life.

There was no belief within me that going through all the chemo, radiation and surgery my doctors were talking about was to become a part of my future and history. Instead, I knew that God had plans for me, and that having cancer, dying from it, and going home, as the doctors were predicting just was not what I was sensing to be my destiny.

We scheduled the MediPort surgery for July 7th, a Monday, so that Mike could be there with me; Mondays were his days off from work. Also, I didn't want to ruin any 4th of July plans that Mike and I had planned, because I had surgery a few days before July Fourth.

July 4, 2008, Friday. A break from it all! By now Mike and I had been running and chasing from one clinic to another or back and forth to the hospital for whatever type of tests the doctors needed, and things were beginning to come to a climax. We needed the weekend to just *chill out*, relax and enjoy the weather and family in celebration of the Fourth of July Holiday. Mike had several days off that weekend, so we went to one of his children to spend the day.

We greatly needed that break from all the tests and to enjoy ourselves before the devastating part of our lives with my chemo treatments began, which was scheduled to start July 18.

July 7, 2008, 7:35 AM Monday: MediPort surgery and liver biopsy–Hartford Hospital. Mike and I went to the Hartford Hospital to get me checked in and ready for the surgery of the MediPort placement and liver biopsy. The hospital had all sorts of construction going on to update and expand the hospital, so there was confusion locating where we had to end up. We finally found the temporary check in area and got me checked in as a day patient.

A nurse took me to a room to get dressed in a fashionable gown and slippers! I was quite well dressed and appealing for the first ever surgery in my life. After I dressed for the surgery, I crawled into my assigned bed, number thirteen! The nurses for both Dr. Jewett and Dr. Crain buzzed in and out and around as they prepared me for the two surgeries. Mike seemed lost; I think he didn't know what to do, or how to handle what was occurring. I suspect he was scared and wished he could snap his fingers to make me healthy and better in an instant!

He looked sad and concerned, and I, oh yes, I had that matter of fact attitude, that this was just another event in my life.

For some reason I did not feel worried or concerned about what was to happen. To me it was a process; nothing more.

I think, at that time, I started to feel strongly that no matter what the biopsy showed; that there was a solution out there somewhere. I wasn't afraid; I was going to discover the solution soon, and all of the commotion with the medical community would be for naught.

There was a cure for me out there – just had to find it!

As we approached July 4th, I had been on the graviola herb for two weeks and been getting my meridians balanced for almost four weeks.

Why did I have the MediPort placed in my body? Not sure. I did a few things mechanically with the medical community mainly because I firmly believed that, for some reason in the future, it would be important to have documentation of various events and the tests for my history.

I knew I was to pass through that time in my life with an entirely different story than my beloved doctors and nurses wrote for me. Just didn't know all the words to it yet.

The nurses and Dr. Jewett did a great job of making our visit jolly and pleasant. I'm now drugged up enough to get moved to the operating room around 10:00 AM. The surgery for the installation of the MediPort in a vein in my left shoulder started at 10:21 AM, ended by 11:22 AM, and by 12:30 PM the biopsy of the liver was completed. Everything went very smoothly. No issues whatsoever with the liver biopsy.

The lab results of the liver biopsy came back as positive for metastatic adenocarcinoma. The tumor sample from the liver had a poorly differentiated appearance with some tubular or ductal formations. The tissue was compared with my right breast carcinoma and was found to be similar to that tumor.

I vaguely remember waking long enough between the two procedures to realize the change of doctors and procedures. The doctor's report said I was awake during the biopsy procedure, but I'm afraid you would have to hypnotize me to remember what happened. Anyway, there didn't seem to be anything eventful for my story for you. Just a procedure so you would know the process for inflammatory breast cancer, I won't bore you anymore with this event.

Barely remember being moved back to the recovery room shortly after the biopsy. I do remember walking with Mike out of the hospital for the car around 3:00 PM, going home and slept off the drugs once I got onto the bed.

July 9, 2008, Wednesday 6:38 AM–West Bend. Called Dr Jewett's clinic about some redness that extended directly below the pocket for the MediPort and set an appointment to go in to have it checked out. He examined the port area and thought there were some signs of some inflammation driven by gravity related to the surgery and no other signs of infection; no significant hematoma or fever.

At the meeting, Dr. Jewett reviewed the liver biopsy results with me, and told me it was positive for metastatic breast cancer and my diagnosis was now changed to stage four!

July 11, 2008, 9:00 AM, Friday: Vince Lombardi clinic, Slinger, Dr Jella. My friend, Ruth, met me at the clinic to be a support and a second pair of ears for me. This was the day of truth; the day that the doctors told me the final verdict of all the testing that was done.

We went over the side effects of the Docetaxel and Herceptin. The Docetaxel potential side effects included but not limited to loss of hair cytopenias, tiredness, fatigue, weight gain, skin changes, nail changes/loss, chemo brain, neuropathy, nausea, and vomiting. From the Herceptin there could be a possible decrease in my cardiac function and that my heart function needed to be monitored once every 3-4 months with a MUGA Scan.

He wanted me to start right away with the chemo treatment and schedule them to start the next day, but I had a sense to stall the start of the treatment. I told him, "I need to get some of my personal affairs and work taken care of before starting the chemo and being unable to work because of the fatigue, nausea and feeling sick." He asked, "We should start the chemo immediately, the sooner the better, so what timeframe are you looking at to get started?" I answered, "Give me about one to two weeks before we start the treatment." We set a date for July 18.

Ruth and I asked a few other questions of Dr. Jella and very likely gave him a difficult time. I remember he appeared stressed. Dr. Jella explained to me the side effects of the chemo treatment, and I asked again the magic question, "What would have been the cause of the cancer? Especially breast cancer, since there is no known family member that has had breast cancer other than one back in the 1950's, and she was exposed to radiation?!

Would it have been my diet, lifestyle, or some other things I would have been exposed to in the past?

Is it related to my father having died of mesothelioma, and because I handled my Dad's laundry and such?"

I was told that there is no precise known cause. He didn't know why I got cancer. It wasn't because my father worked with asbestos and my having breathed in some particles when I handled his laundry or hugged him.

Dr. Jella had done everything within his power to answer all of my unusual questions, to have compassion for me and my dilemma, and to keep me aware of the statistical outcome for me. I'm grateful that he was my doctor and was willing to listen to what I did and thought of doing as an alternative or in addition to his recommendations to save my life.

In spite of their efforts; I felt that there was something in the works. Dr. Jella had no idea what was to come, and nor did I, exactly! The dilemma was just a bump in the road, a small detour, or debris on the dance floor that throws off your step a little. My attitude was rapidly becoming more concrete about my future outcome, and I'm sure I frustrated the doctors and their staff. But I just knew I was going to survive and could not give the idea of death any substance.

Ruth still cannot dismiss how I handled the appointment. She was awe struck by my behavior, and I'm sure that if she was amazed, then surely Dr. Jella either thought I was delusional or crazy. At least thought that this woman in his exam room was crazy with denial of what he believed was going to be my destiny.

He had no idea what was about to become a part of his legacy.

I knew what he was trying to tell me, and Ruth was impressed that I matter-of-factly took notes and *discussed* my future with him as though we were at a board meeting! Although Dr. Jella tried very hard to prepare me for what was my statistical outcome; I wasn't about to accept the power of his words. I knew better! I KNEW my destiny was to be something other than the picture of doom and gloom the doctors knew to be the normal outcome for someone such as me with stage four inflammatory breast cancer that had metastasized.

Dr. Jella had again explained to me, "You will have to have chemo for at least twelve months. After that we will run some tests and discuss how well the chemo treatments worked to slow the growth of the tumor in your breast. That's the best we can hope to have happen. If lucky, the tumor will be dead. If so, then we will do surgery to remove the dead or stopped tumors along with the whole breast. We'll discuss the reconstructing of the breast at the same time, and somewhere during that time we'll decide on when and if radiation should be done."

At one point of our discussion I asked, "Do I understand you correctly, that when I am thirty years older.....?" He shook his head from left to right and said, "NO, NO, NO, you will never live that long!"

Three years down and 27 or more years to go! It's a contest now.

Statistics I found for inflammatory breast cancer showed that there was a significantly less than ten percent survival rate regardless of stage of the cancer. So statistically, Dr. Jella would have been accurate with his statement of me having a short remaining life. However, he nor any of the other doctors ever expected me to do so exceptionally well or to blow away all the numbers for IBC and cancer as a whole.

Ruth still gets excited about her experience from that appointment. My attitude when I left that appointment was that of *knowing that I was going to survive* regardless of what everyone said or thought.

Yet I went through the expected motions to get rid of things, closed down my business except for a few of my clients, and arranged whatever possible for my death should my *knowing* be wrong. Besides, should I overcome the cancer as I was beginning to believe would be the case, I can always buy new furniture, car, and restart my college financial planning business.

Chapter Ten

Fifth Messenger From God

God Can't Do Everything,
But He Can Do Some Important Things.

July 15, 2008, Tuesday: Vince Lombardi Clinic, Slinger met with Pat, a social worker at the clinic, by phone. Pat was requested by the nursing staff at the Vince Lombardi clinic to contact me as I had expressed a concern whether or not I should relocate to Arizona or Southern California. The doctors strongly felt that I should have been closer to my family during the last stage of my life.

Since I had not worked as of the beginning of May I was running out of money and had to initiate a research for resources for help. Before Pat called me, I had questioned the nurses what they thought of the concerns of the doctors regarding my needs as the cancer progressed. I had already sold off my possessions, or gave them away, because I did not want to leave these behind for my family and friends to deal with should the end come before expected, and in the event I didn't get the miracle I had received. Inflammatory breast cancer is a rapid and aggressive killer which leaves the person (male or female) little time to prepare, so I had acted quickly.

If I relocated closer to my family, I would need to make certain that my insurance, doctors and resources were in alignment before leaving for there. I was happy that Pat had called me with some resources to help in making my decision. It was a tough emotional decision. I wanted to be close to my kids and Mike, but I was extremely torn with which way to move with the pressure from the doctors. I had a hard choice to make and I couldn't determine what the right direction should have been. My life was in Wisconsin, my business was in Wisconsin, and yet I saw the reasoning to be close to my kids.

July 15, 2008 Tuesday, the last messenger. Another friend and client named, Kathy, happened to call. Totally unexpected and timely. Kathy and I had not had contact for almost three years! I've known Kathy since our babies started grade school! We got each other caught up on events in our lives and it was now my turn to tell her about the latest thing going on in my life; the cancer.

Kathy told me of this fantastic person she had known for years who had helped quite a large number of cancer victims who had been through the whole process of chemo, surgery, radiation and whatever else their diagnosis required to save their lives, then ultimately be told by the doctors to get their affairs in order because there was nothing else that the doctors could do anymore to save their lives.

Kathy was very excited about this woman's personalized program that had caused all the cancer victims to still be alive five, ten, and twenty years beyond the sentence of death! Kathy explained to me that this woman was in the Madison area, and that's when it finally clicked in my head that the woman that Kathy was excited about helping me might be Marcia Simler!

I asked Kathy, "Is this woman's name Marcia Simler, and is her business called Natural Health Works in Madison?" She said, "Yes!" and I responded with, "Oh, My God! I know who you are talking about! Three other people had told me about her during the past six months of this year! I'll call her right after I walk back to the house and we end our phone call. I don't need to be hit over the head more than four times by God to get the message that I'm supposed to call her and do what she tells me to do to get rid of the cancer!" We laughed and giggled about the oddity of the other three messengers and Kathy's message, and how the other three messengers were presented to me.

This was my fourth message from God to call Marcia. Sometimes I can be a little slow and unaware of God sending me my *rescuer to save me from drowning.* I'm just happy that He continued to send me messengers of help before I died the horrible death process of inflammatory breast cancer during chemo, radiation, and......! Not like the story I told you about earlier where a man was sent two boats to save him from drowning before he died in the water! I was sent a huge *yacht*!! And I recognized that the *yacht* was there for my rescue.

I grabbed my *yacht* immediately that same day. Now I knew how I was supposed to fix the problem! How I was going to get my cure. Never considered it a miracle at that time until other persons, as they heard parts of my story of my cure, called me a *miracle*! I was just on a mission to find what God wanted me to do, and do it without question.

After I was done talking with Kathy and walking my dog, Jake, I called Marcia, introduced myself and told her how I got her name and information. She was impressed that four different people she worked with throughout the state of Wisconsin knew me and introduced her to me! She was amazed that she was referred to me by two of the people before I had the slightest indication of cancer, and that this had occurred during January to April 2008!!

I explained to her a little about my life event I was experiencing at the time. I gave her just enough information to let her understand the severity, and where I was in the process of all the tests. That the chemo was scheduled to start July 18. I let her know that I was being put through all the tests to determine what type of cancer I had, that the doctors were considering the diagnosis could be breast cancer, and the doctors were just about finished with their determination of my prognosis. I didn't tell her which breast or which tests that they put me through. I wanted to test her abilities, so I didn't give her too much detail.

During our rapid conversation, Marcia wanted to know, "What blood type are you?" "A" "Had you started chemo or any other treatments for the cancer?" I said, "I had been put through all the possible tests one can experience for cancer, such as the PET Scan, blood tests, MRI's and whatever other test they can think of to run on me. They are still working on the final diagnosis."

Marcia explained to me, "You have cancer because your body is too acidic, besides being nutritionally deficient and imbalanced." She said, "Cancer loves an acidic environment, but cannot survive in an alkaline environment. It dies in an alkaline body. Once we convert your body to a more pH balanced and alkaline environment, as well as build up your immune system, the cancer will be gone in four weeks."

Well, that was extraordinary news!

I told her, "You have the job!"

And asked Marcia, "What do you want me to do? What is the next step?" Her answer was, "I'll start you on the ZetaMax which I'll ship out to you tomorrow, along with a saliva kit to get a sample from you and you send it to the address on the kit right away. OK?"

"Sounds great! What can I start doing in the meantime while I'm waiting for the ZetaMax package and the results from the saliva test? The chemo treatments start July 18, so I'd like to start something right away without waiting." Marcia said, "Start adding lemon to your water, eat watermelon and seedless grapes which are very alkalizing for Type A's along with the ZetaMax. They will get you started towards being more alkaline, and I will email you a Type A food list." Which I did consume one or the other, or all, on a daily basis. I still do.

I drank at least 128 oz. of purified (definitely filtered) water daily in which I had put the juice, oil and peel of *one* squeezed lemon to flavor the water and to keep my blood Type A body alkalized.

Marcia instructed me in which foods to start eating immediately and stop eating to start balancing my alkalinity. She also stated, "The ZetaMax contains the core chemicals of 60 minerals, 28 vitamins, and 3 essential fatty acids, and 12 amino acids that each body needs every day to rebuild and maintain balance. Each body I work with, whether human, horse, dog, cat or other animal, gets put on ZetaMax to provide them with the basic chemicals they need to be healthy." Along with the ZetaMax, a "saliva kit" and information was sent to me. I was to collect some of my saliva on the enclosed cotton swab, fill out the form, and mail it the next day to her clinic in Monroe, Wisconsin; which I did.

Marcia had emailed to me a list of foods that are considered "beneficial", "neutral" and "avoid" to a Type A body. Her lists for Type B, AB or O have the same categories, however the foods listed in each category can and are different from one type to another. She also told me which foods are especially poisonous to me and to start avoiding them more than ninety percent of the time, such as:

Wheat
Corn
All potatoes
All Peppers
Tomatoes
Red Meat
Pork
Oranges
Bananas
Cow's Milk and products

As we talked, I became hopeful, and believed that Marcia was an answer to the prayers of many. How could she not be my answer? Consider the number of people, who did not know one another, that told me about her in the period of six months in the same year!

I had kept in mind that the Bible states in Genesis that God said everything our bodies need to keep it healthy and to heal it are in our plant life. Therefore, I did the saliva swab test the morning after the overnight package from Marcia arrived. The saliva test would help us learn what my chemical makeup was before the first chemo treatment would begin on July 18. It was important to me to know what my body was doing before the chemo. I wanted a test result before the chemo started because it would help determine exactly what my body needed to heal itself, what was needed to fix the source of the problem, not just the symptom. I wanted a test result unaffected by the influence of the chemo. I believed the answer to my dilemma was in what I was consuming, and I needed to find out exactly how to correct what I was doing wrong.

A few days after that eventful phone call, Marcia and I spoke a second time on the phone about how to get healed. She started with the results of my saliva sample I had mailed her. The numbers were the lowest she had ever seen anyone have for their results.

Amazed as I was that I had cancer when this journey began, I was more amazed to learn that I had the lowest numbers she had ever seen come in her clinic over the twenty plus years she had been in business. Apparently, zero percent is death and the majority of my numbers averaged five to ten percent which indicated how well my spleen, pancreas, gallbladder, liver and others functioned! My small intestine was at fifteen percent. My large intestine was functioning at twenty percent capacity. I had two viruses, three parasites, two bad bacteria, nine chemicals, three infections, and seven heavy metals to indicate a few of the test results from July 2008.

That second phone call in July of 2008, about a week prior to my first chemo was an interesting and exhilarating conversation. Marcia was in her educative mode. She told me how cancer is considered a virus; hence the fact that there were two viruses in my system did not surprise me. Next, she told me that all of my *congestion* was located in my right breast, all of my surrounding lymph nodes from my thyroid down and around my breast and up into my right armpit were affected along with my liver. I was shocked she identified the areas in my body affected by the viruses that I had to ask her, "How did you know!? I didn't tell you where the cancer was found! I only told you that the doctors were testing me for breast cancer!"

Marcia answered, "Based on the results of the saliva test she was able to determine the location of the affected areas of my body, by the way the chemical results and percentage levels of the organs turned out."

Had the congestion, for instance, been on my upper left the results would have been different from what they actually were for my right. Similarly, had the numbers again been different for another part of the body, Marcia would have been able to determine which other part of the body was affected, how it was affected, and what then needed to be done to help the body repair itself.

You see, each and every thing is a living *chemical beaker* of its own unique chemical design and never exactly matching that of another person. You and I can both be Blood Type A, the beginning of each of our *chemical beaker's* mixture, however each will both ultimately be different.

You may think that you have no sensitivities to any of the food or drink that you dump into your beaker, however in time any of the negative reactions you probably unknowingly had in the past will catch up to you. Let's say that you love hot cocoa milk. OK, maybe you don't. But anyway, every time that you drink the chocolate milk, it goes down deliciously well! You notice no reaction to any of the chemicals you have just consumed. Our bodies are extremely adaptable to whatever we do to it while it is in its prime state of health. Let's imagine your body's chemistry can't accept the chocolate but it can accept the cow's milk, sugar, marshmallows, etc. However, because you were unaware of your intolerance to the chocolate your body expends more of its resources to prevent a negative reaction to the chocolate, also known as an allergic reaction, and to keep you alive.

As time passes and you continue to consume chocolate (dumped it into your beaker) your body loses the capacity to overcome the chemical reaction caused by the chocolate in your body (beaker). Voila! You now have an allergy to the chocolate which ultimately will cause damage to your body. The reaction will either be internal or external, showing up in some manner either visible or never noticeable to you at all. Now you start developing disorders, then major diseases. The process can take years to develop a sensitivity to food.

More time passes as you continue to put those chemicals into your beaker without awareness of whether it is *Beneficial* or *Neutral* to your chemistry. Even more serious, damaging and disease causing, is the consumption of chemicals (food and drink, etc.) into your body that are from your *Avoid* category. Just as in chemistry class in school, we were taught by our chemistry teacher which chemicals could cause an explosion when mixed and which would cause a wonderful end product when mixed with the chemicals in the beaker (your body). SAME THING!!

This is how we end up with most of our diseases and disorders of the body. We burn up our body's ability and capacity to fight off nasty chemicals, heavy metals, viruses and parasites as well as keep its adaptability (immune system) high to what we are doing to it daily. We start having numerous colds, flu, diabetes, cancer, muscular and nerve damage, to name a few.

So, it's your choice. Either continue doing what you're doing and die a horrible death, or learn how to better care for your home, your body temple, so that it will be able to serve you on your life's mission.

Chapter Eleven

God Was Still Covering My Back

July 17, 2008, Thursday met with Dr. Jewett: Vince Lombardi Clinic in Slinger. A follow-up on the MediPort placement. The next day I was scheduled for my first chemo.

July 18, 2008, Friday: Vince Lombardi Clinic in Slinger. First Scheduled Day of Chemo.

Mike was on vacation that week, and it was his birthday, so he was able to take me to the clinic, which was a good thing. Driving yourself and chemo treatments don't mix well, at all! The patient is too intoxicated from all the drugs to perform the infusion that the danger is too great to drive. That Friday, God was working overtime.

We checked in at the receptionist for my first chemo infusion and my appointment with Dr. Jella for a status update type of exam before the chemo started. The nurse came for me and we all went into the common area where I chose a recliner to get settled in and started. The nurse attached the tubing and was able to flush the MediPort but was unable to draw any blood for the lab work they needed to do before starting the infusion. I could feel a very small sensation below my sternum as well as noticed my heart beating a bit more than usual as they did the flushing; however there was no blood draw.

Because the nurses couldn't get the MediPort to work, they quickly sent me from the clinic directly to the hospital to have a dye study done to determine why the MediPort refused to work. If the staff at the hospital could get the port to work the plan was to still do my first chemo on July 18th.

Mike drove me to the hospital and waited for me in the waiting room. I was grateful I didn't have to wait around for one of the hospital shuttles or taxis. Having to travel from one location to another and back again would have been an annoying commotion.

When I realized that the contrast they wanted to use for the test might contain iodine, the hospital staff decided not to proceed with the test because of the family iodine sensitivity. Iodine had caused my father to die on the surgical table three times before they stopped giving Dad the iodine dye. Iodine has been known to make me ill also. So the staff refused to do the tests on the MediPort.

Instead the hospital staff sent me back to the clinic; no one was certain whether to send me home or back to the clinic since the hospital couldn't run the tests. As Mike and I headed back to the clinic, the hospital staff called in a prescription to the pharmacy that I was to take over the weekend to premedicate myself so I would be able to have the dye study on Monday morning. The dye study meant taking x-rays and a video x-ray to establish the placement and function issues of the MediPort.

Once back at the clinic, Nurse Susan and I discussed my feelings and fears regarding the chemo. She answered my questions for approximately thirty minutes about the chemo treatments as well as the dye study that was to occur on Monday, July 21st.

Sue asked me to call her later in the day, which I did. I was stressed and upset that day about the delay to get started, the pressure from people to get started, and afraid of the chemo process and what to expect from getting chemo treatments. And yet, I was excited about having started a small portion of the program that Marcia designed for me.

Do I stall or do I proceed with the chemo?

Do I do both Marcia's program and my oncologist's program together?

Do I do only the one or the other?

Anyway, Sue was concerned that I understood our conversation that we just had. She wanted to make certain that I had accepted the information about the chemo and premed schedule for the MediPort failure study on the following Monday.

Sue was assured that I understood everything we discussed, but I told her I was not ready to start the chemo treatment on Monday as they expected. For some reason I was not emotionally up to starting the chemo. Everything seemed to happen so fast to me. Others around me got upset that I didn't have a mastectomy done in May. To me something of the puzzle was missing. Besides, I had just spoken with Marcia Simler on July 15th. As a result, the 1st chemo treatment was rescheduled for Friday, July 25th, the following Friday.

Delayed a week.

God was up to something, could sense being led towards a different area of the dance floor.

Blood was drawn for labs that Friday, the 18th, and my cancer antigen 27.29 level was at 73.1. The cancer antigen level, a marker for cancer, increased from 58.4 on June 4th to 73.1.

And, maybe it didn't increase!? It could actually have been on its way down from a higher level because I had already been working on alkalizing my body and strictly ate what I should have eaten and avoided what I should not eat at least ninety percent of the time.

Chapter Twelve

Complimentary Solutions

Marcia Simler and everyone that worked in her clinics, Natural Health Works, were excited that I came to them when I did. Usually, the cancer patients that arrived on her doorstep would be those who had gone through all the process of chemo, radiation, surgery, reconstruction, and whatever else needed to save their lives; then be told by the doctors that they couldn't do anything more for them to save their lives. So they were excited to work with someone who was at the beginning of this chemo process instead of someone who hadn't gone through all of the surgery, chemo and radiation.

Marcia tests 80 points thru Kinesiology to determine what needs to be cleansed, balanced or detoxed. She personally designs the best diet for people who come to her and gives them a summary sheet which includes *beneficial foods*, *neutral foods*, and *avoid foods*. Because Kinesiology takes the guessing out of what exactly your body is in need of to heal and maintain itself, your body heals faster, and you save money.

Viruses can be, and are, pre-cancer. Marcia and her team check which plan is beneficial for your body's healing, prevention and maintenance. Marcia and her staff believe we should use what God provided for us instead of drugging up our bodies or cutting it out.

After briefly talking with Marcia on July 15th, Marcia made certain to ship a bottle of ZetaMax, which I mentioned before, that contains the 60 minerals, 28 vitamins, 3 essential fatty acids, and 12 amino acids that every person needs for their body. Because without this basic combination of chemicals we develop a deficiency, which becomes a disorder which then turns into a disease, and ultimately an early and messy death!

ZetaMax acts as a base to start designing a personal program upon which she adds any other herbs and supplements the body needs.

July 19, 2008, Saturday. Mailed my first salvia sample to Marcia Simler.

Now things are starting to get exciting. The package containing a saliva kit and some information came the day before in the mail from Marcia. As soon as I crawled out of bed that morning; before drinking, eating, or brushing my teeth, I got out the kit, took out the cotton swab, and swabbed my lower gums and under my tongue to saturate the swab. Sealed it in the mailing baggy and later went to the Post Office to make sure I had enough postage on the envelope and be hand stamped. Did not want it to come back because of a lack of postage, you know! Or, worse, have it get jammed and torn apart in the one of the postage machines and disposed of by the post office. So off the saliva sample went to its destination in Madison.

July 21, 2008 8:37 AM, Monday. Dr. Martin Crain: Hartford Hospital again.

Mike and I arrived at the hospital, and I was quickly led to the area where the staff would run their tests on me. Mike waited for me in the waiting room.

Dr. Crain found a dense partial fibrin sheath near the tip of the port catheter as well as a retrograde flow and put me on a prescription to dissolve the sheath.

In my opinion, this was another delay which prevented my leaping into having a mastectomy when I was first told I had cancer or starting with the cancer treatment process before I did. God was definitely watching over me and my every dance step! The MediPort delay was an eventful occurrence. At least, I think it was eventful enough to allow me more time to implement the personalized program Marcia had worked up for me. The first chemo infusion was definitely moved off to July 25th.

Remember, I had just started some of my personalized repair program for my body as Marcia had directed me in our first phone conversation a few days before, on the 15th. I was excited and relieved that the port would not work when it was supposed to on July 18. This gave me a few days to eat some of the foods Marcia recommended and avoid those she had on my avoid ninety percent of the time category from my daily nutrition.

After Mike and I arrived home, and as we walked up to the front door, I spotted a package left by UPS on the porch. Looking at the label I noticed the return address said it was from Marcia. I was immediately in "7th Heaven"! It contained the "liquid gold", which Marcia calls ZetaMax, which is the base of the chemicals/nutrition every living body needs to be healthy.

Such perfect timing!

The MediPort still wasn't working!

Chemo was pushed off to Friday, July 25th; nearly a week later.

And now my 1st care package from Marcia arrived on the same day as my trip back to the hospital to get the MediPort to work!

Halleluiah!! It became a fantastic day! More than I realized at the time, but I was suspecting something was in the making!

The MediPort failure borrowed an extra week for me to implement my body's personalized repair program that Marcia designed. The doctors couldn't get upset nor panicky with me should it have been my choice to wait a week.

Chapter Thirteen

Power of Prayer

July 22, 2008, Tuesday-Kanelechi Kamah, her friend and I prayed that evening.

It was late. Maybe around 9:00 pm when Kanelechi had phoned to see how I was doing and what the latest news was at the time. After getting caught up to date with some chatter and giggles, we thought it would be a great idea to pray for a cure. One of Kanelechi's friends, who is a prayer warrior as well as Kanelechi, was at her home.

I believe that the three of us had prayed for about an hour or more. Kanelechi, her friend and I invoked the blessings and graces of God to provide me with a cure. As they prayed via her phone at her home, I sat at the kitchen table, the ear headset for my cellular phone tightly fitted in my ear, asked God to hear our prayer.

As I sat at the table with my face in my hands our prayer that night felt very powerful. I could feel my skin react with goose bumps (chills) as we asked God for His cure. Kanelechi and her friend were deep in their prayer, asking God to cure me. With my face still in my hands, I whispered, "In Jesus' Name", and at the same time asked Jesus and God to hear our prayer; to hear our request to destroy the cancer and make my body perfectly healthy. As we prayed, I actually felt as though Jesus had placed

His arm around my shoulders as He stood over me, in His red and white robes, at the kitchen table to comfort me, trying to have me feel as though everything would be perfectly fine as He softly told me, "Everything will be OK?".

Kanelechi and I ended our prayer in tears and ecstasy. We talked a little longer, and finally, we both agreed that it was well past bedtime. That night I felt overwhelmed with peace, happiness, and joy from the prayer.

Whenever Kanelechi and I would pray for any of our needs or those of someone else, we would feel such unexplainable happiness after we finished. That night that feeling was stronger than ever before. We have learned that whenever we miss a few days of prayer that things start to go wrong. Interesting!! But very true!!

Of course, as I prepared for bed, I had to examine myself to see if there had been any change whatsoever. It was difficult to spot any further improvement than what had already occurred from visiting Dr. Ron, from the visualization of the "laser beams" killing any cancer cells and taking the graviola for close to a month. Before that night the only improvement that I had noticed over the past week was a slightly less hard breast, and that maybe the tumor had stopped increasing as rapidly as it had been since the biopsy in May. The tumor in my breast had grown an additional 2-3 cm, which made it approximately 6 cm by early July. My tumor in my breast was showing some small signs of slower growth rate.

As I picked up my rosary from the dresser, I held the crucifix in my hand, kissed it, thanked Jesus for bringing Kanelechi, her friend and I together in prayer. Jesus was also thanked for putting

His arm around my shoulders as we prayed, and for all the other times He held me as I went to sleep each night.

July 23, 2008, late sunrise of the next morning.

It was time to get up and get out of bed to tackle the new day head on. But before I got out of bed, I looked for my rosary which was still in the same hand as when I went to sleep. While I held the cross in my hand, I thanked Jesus for dying on the cross for us. Thanked God for my friends who helped me through the journey of transformation. Once again thanked God for bringing Kanelechi, her friend and I together in prayer for a cure.

My rosary was placed safely under my pillow for later when I'd go to bed that night. I was being a little lazy that morning, nicely tucked in the comfort of my cocoon of quilt and blankets. I know; a quilt in July! Seems out of season, but what can I say? I like being warm at night instead of chilled. As I remembered the memories created from the night before I had decided to see if there was a change or not to my breast. There was this compelling urge to find an expected change; yet, I was immensely surprised to find my breast soft as it should be when healthy, and half the size from where it had grown to since the biopsy in May!

"Oh, My God!!" What an understatement!! I exclaimed in a loud whisper, "The tumor had decreased in size by half!" My emotions at the time were indescribably grateful and HAPPY!!!

I was so happy with this change that I couldn't contain myself and had to call Kanelechi and some of my family and friends to let them know of the dramatic change!

The next day's morning, Thursday, the tumor in my breast had reduced significantly more, so much so that the tumor was nearly gone by Friday morning, July 25th! It was wonderful to be able to cinch my bra back to the original hooks I used before this all started! I had been seriously considering whether it was prudent to buy a larger bra to accommodate the increased size of my breast. There were no additional hooks to loosen the bra any further.

Friday morning, July 25th, my breast was back to normal and I was unable to feel any of my congested lymph nodes! Now what do I do? Do I go to the clinic or forget it altogether? What do I do? I couldn't see or feel any reason to go for the first chemo. I constantly debated whether or not to go to the clinic as I showered and prepared to leave for the clinic. Mike was at work and unreachable to discuss it with him. Finally, I decided I needed to go since the MediPort that was placed July 7th was now certainly due for a flushing on the 25th which I was told needed to be done every four weeks. Besides, it was scheduled for a follow up from its failure to function a week before. So I went. If it weren't for that reason, I would not have gone to the clinic for the chemo treatment at all! Why should I? My feelings and thoughts were that it was no longer logical to do chemo. But I wanted documented proof also, to be able to tell the world.

July 25, 2008 10:00 AM–3:50 PM, Friday, at Vince Lombardi Clinic in Slinger. First Chemo infusion.

Being nervous and scared, I was still excited about going. I wanted Dr. Jella to examine me because of the huge change. I wanted to tell him my story after he did his exam where he'd find out that the tumor was gone! Ugh! He was not there! Hadn't realized that Dr. Jella wasn't scheduled to see me that day, and that he wasn't scheduled to be at the clinic either. He was either off or at a clinic in Milwaukee. Of course! I didn't think! He wasn't expecting any need to see me to have me scheduled for an appointment. I was only to start my chemo. Now what?

Disappointed, I allowed myself to be led to one of the infusion areas with the reclining chair. These are almost as comfy as a bed! Each area had its own suspended TV. There were puzzle tables, scrapbooking supplies, magazines, games; just about everything one could think of to keep you entertained while attached one of the infusion machines for several hours. This was all very nice, and the nurses were very kind, but I just wanted to get my MediPort flushed and leave.

I let them attach the I.V. equipment. As they were flushing the port, and drawing blood for lab work, I had indicated that I was not interested in doing chemo that day, and I just wanted to see Dr. Jella.

I wanted him to see the change that occurred before informing the nurses or anyone at the clinic. I had a fantastic story to tell and I wanted him to be the first to hear what I had to show and tell! Now it had to wait. The nurses were in a tizzy! WHAT!!?? NO CHEMO!!?? One would have thought I had shot off a gun! WHEW!

I knew what had happened to me. However, I was not about to tell them of the reduction of the tumor. It was important to have Dr. Jella do an exam without any preconceived ideas from me, or his nurses. He needed to examine me without knowing of the reduction in my tumor. It was important to get his honest and spontaneous reaction to this miracle! No one had coached me as to how to handle a miracle; I just sensed that it was important at the time to handle the events that way.

The nurses *panicked*. One of them left to contact Dr. Jella. As I'm sitting in one of the recliners, hooked up to the I.V. machine, several of them came back to talk with me. They said Dr. Jella was adamant that I had to do chemo because my cancer antigen level had increased from 58.4 to 73.1.

My day went from elation to disappointment that I couldn't share my miracle with them that day and, finally, to panic and fear that maybe they were right, and I was not. That there was no miracle that week. Something however bothered me. Something didn't seem to connect or be correct. I wasn't sure what to think with the news of the increase of the cancer antigen level; because I knew that the cancer antigen level can be used as a marker indicating whether or not there is cancer in one's body. How could the level have increased to 73.1?

Hadn't I just received a miracle?!

What was not disclosed to me was the fact that the 73.1 marker was from a lab test taken earlier in July, and not from the lab work they had just done that day, July 25th.

Maybe the lab results from that day showed something which, regardless of the fact that my tumors in my lymph nodes and breast were gone, conflicted to sight and touch. After all there was my liver hiding behind my rib cage that no one could see or touch to know how it was at the time. I was confused. I had to make a decision on the spot. The nurses were kind, but I felt pressured. Scared. I resigned to their concerns.

Grudgingly I allowed myself to do the chemo. I accepted a thought that by resigning to do the chemo, I would do it up to three times. Well, since I settled to do chemo I would absolutely only do it for no more than six times. That's all, and no more, I thought to myself. *That's exactly how many times I did do chemo.* At the time, I had no idea that I was predicting what was to come.

I went from expecting my life over the next three years to be a process consumed with doing chemo a minimum of twelve months, evaluate the status of the tumors after the twelve months, do a mastectomy and reconstruction, if possible after that, and radiation; to this unbelievable miraculous event. Every bit of the information I found on the internet indicated that the survival of someone with inflammatory breast cancer is approximately five percent and less than a year from its onset regardless of stage the person is at when diagnosed. Now what do I do?

It wasn't until several months had passed, when I got a copy of my medical records, that I had learned the date of the 73.1 cancer antigen level was from an older date. If I had known the date, and not assumed the date of the 73.1 level was from July 25th, I strongly believe that I would not have done chemo at all on the 25th. Why? The stories I had heard about chemo were scary. The sickness, chemo brain and fatigue I had from the six times of chemo and the three months of tests had really messed up my life.

It's hard for me to imagine someone diagnosed with cancer experiencing the full-blown process, as we knew it at the time I wrote *Being Held By God*, of eradicating a cancer in the body. Just can't! I know I would never have completed the full cycle of getting rid of mine that the doctors talked of for me. NOPE! My quality of life during the tests, and the chemo I did experience, were enough for me and Mike! I would have put an end to the chemo process by the second chemo, if God had not led me to the resources, He did, which caused my events to have been different than they were predicted to be by statistics. I firmly believe the program that Marcia had put me on made the chemo process less difficult.

I fully understand now how someone going through the process of trying to rescue one's life from cancer ends up losing family and friends. There is so much fear associated with cancer. Mainly, the fear of contracting the disease just by being in the same space as the cancer victim, and the fear of knowing how to "handle it" and being a part of that moment in history with the cancer victim is too stressful. So much so that it tears apart the cancer victim and reduces their ability to fight it.

Along with loosing relationships, a cancer patient especially suffers from losing financial stability affecting the quality of life of themselves and their families, along with mental and emotional well-being. Their overall health to function normally as a healthy person is compromised, again reducing the quality of life. I truly believe many don't make it through the process because they give up the fight as their lives are turned upside down and destroyed by the cancer process as a whole. One's attitude shifts from fighting for your life to "what is the point?"

"There is no quality of life."

"I'd rather die, than continue this regimen, this process...."

"I've lost my appearance. My health has to get worse before it gets better?"

"There are family and friends who have abandoned me when I need them the most.... what is the purpose of all of it?"

"What is the benefit to me or anyone that knows me, or doesn't?"

If it hadn't been for the fact that *I knew with all of my soul and heart* that God had plans for me, there would not have been the miracle. If I had not listened to His messengers, there would not have been the miracle. If I had not opened my heart and mind to the messages He sent me throughout this whole journey, there would not have been this miracle; nor *Being Held By God* to help you. I learned to let God into my life during that part of my journey. Consequently, God had sent me to help you learn how to create your own miracles. How what I did can help you to overcome cancer, and some of the other major disorders of our bodies by implementing the resources I've used.

There are many other legitimate complimentary therapies out there in addition to the ones I've included in *Being Held By God*. The ones I've used tremendously helped me to tolerate the six chemo times, as well as kept me looking very healthy, and reduced the cancer process expected for me to the six infusions and follow up exams and tests.

Anyway, after I completed the first chemo infusion Mike took me home. I kept it in my mind that I'm only doing chemo three to six times, with six chemo treatments being the maximum. When we got home, I dragged myself upstairs to go to bed to sleep for hours.

Week one of the three-week cycle was a week of extreme fatigue, sleep, and my body purged the toxins of the chemo. I tried my hardest to function normally. I had to muster up every effort to just sit somewhere or lie on the sofa and keep my eyes open to watch TV.

In the second week, the effects of the first week were less debilitating.

Sunday of the third week of the first cycle, as I took my shower, strands of hair ended up in my hands. Reluctantly, and as-a-matter-of process I got the scissors, and without ceremony cut my hair down to one-half inch so my lost hair wouldn't clog the drains or leave hair in unwanted places. From that point on I wore one of my wigs *all* the time.

Chapter Fourteen

New Birth Day

Aug. 15, 2008, 10:00 AM-3:50 PM Friday: Vince Lombardi Clinic, Slinger. It was the Second chemo date.

The lab nurse drew blood to run the tests to see if it would be OK to do the chemo infusion. We also talked about redoing the test for the cancer antigen level. The nurse drew a vial for that test, in the event that it would be decided to be done.

Anyway, the test got rejected. Doctor Jella thought it was not timely. Of course, he would have made that decision. How thoughtless of me! Dr. Jella had no idea about what was about to happen to him and his nurse that day. Why would he have agreed to such a costly blood test as the cancer antigen level test, when he didn't see me on July 25th or hear anything about my dramatic repair! I certainly wasn't thinking at the time as to the chain of command or the insurance process when I asked the lab nurse to draw the extra vial of blood, which got tossed. Oh, well! Live and learn!

Doctor Jella came into the examination room, and we exchanged the usual greetings and handshake. Talked about how I was doing, and about the chemo that was to be done. We spent a little time on the effects of the chemo from the first time; that it had made me really sick and fatigued for two weeks. I questioned the doses that were given on July 25th and indicated that if they chose to increase the doses, or gave me the same dose, I would have walked out the door, because I couldn't handle the effects of the first time; it was really rough. I told Dr. Jella, and his nurse (Heidi), "I couldn't tolerate it being worse. I couldn't tolerate the first time". The first one and one-half weeks after that chemo infusion left me so fatigued, sick and unable to function. My feelings during recovery from the first chemo were of sympathy and remorse for other cancer sufferers, and the family taking care of this person probably feeling trapped in so many ways. Everyone involved is trapped.

In fact, this sense of remorse intensified for other cancer patients as I went through those six chemo infusions. You see, although I only did those six chemo infusions, they were enough to hinder my ability to work for nearly two weeks out of each three-week cycle.

The first week of the three was just recovery from the infusion of chemicals which meant I slept or was fatigued on the sofa or in bed. I wouldn't drive to or from the clinic, nor drive during the first week and one-half of the cycle because of the fatigue.

During the first and second weeks of the cycle I was affected by chemo brain, fatigue, diarrhea and some nausea. Because of the chemo brain I had difficulty remembering that I had spoken with someone about a client file and what the discussion was about that I ended up calling back the person during my third week to retract what we discussed for my client. That had happened more than once. For some reason the chemo affected the part of my brain that performed any mathematical and financial process. I had decided I had to put more of my financial work on hold until I was in recovery from the chemo. I did not want to cause any financial harm to my clients.

The second week I could begin to think of the possibility of functioning normally, or at least I thought I was functioning more normally. I still experienced the chemo brain, fatigue, diarrhea and some nausea, however at a lesser degree.

Other times during my third week I had it on my mind to complete some work on a file, I pulled out the file during the third week, and found that I completed the work and could not remember anything about when, where, or that I had done the activity. I flipped through the file in complete wonderment at when I did the work! My third week usually amounted to being able to function somewhat normally for my work from Monday through Thursday, as well as feel normal enough to do errands, go shopping, and see friends, whatever I would have done before the chemo. Because Friday I had to return for the infusion again, which started the cycle of uselessness all over again, I had to cram three weeks of functionality into four days.

For me, many of my clients dropped away when they were told of the type of diagnosis I was given. In their mind, you see, I was supposed to have died three years ago. That's what they were expecting to happen to me. I was too great of a risk to work with them. My clients and companies I worked with began to tell me to get back to them after I was done with the chemo and recovered from the cancer; "just focus on getting your health back. We can talk then."

Because of the impact on me from the first infusion, you can understand why I was after a lesser dosage that day; definitely less than last time. A doubled dose was out of the question. I had heard a doubled dose was usually the procedure. As a result it was already in my mind that if he would have given me the same dosages or greater, I would have chosen death over chemo if that were my only true option. I would have headed out the door! That's why I questioned Dr. Jella about my dosages for the first infusion. I felt I needed some control over how sick and incapacitated I became from the chemo, and to have control over my life during those first two weeks of each cycle. I would have taken my chances with what was a definite disappearance of the tumors. To me, my mindset was that my tumors were all gone! Then, as well as later, I just wanted the medical tests done to have proof and documentation of what had happened.

Because there had been a huge change since he last examined me on July 18, I kept a straight face and with a hint towards indicating something had developed with my breast but with a calm tone of voice so as not to give away the surprise; I told him, "Before you decide the doses to give me, you need to check me out." His body language said, "Why?" Which was understandable, but I pressed forward.

I gave him, nor any of the nurses, any indication or clue of what he would find. I know; I was being deceptive.

With a little more convincing tone to my voice, I restated, "You need to check me out before going any further." Dr. Jella considered what I said; he relentlessly came over to me where I sat on the exam room chair.

I started to lift my tank top for my right side but realized he was going to examine me without lifting my top. He began to press around my armpit and lymph nodes on my right side. Heidi, his nurse, observed. He lifted my arm higher and pressed around more, and a puzzled look appeared on his face. I found I had a hard time to not show any excitement or emotion.

He moved around the chair to my left side and began to press around that armpit and the lymph node areas on my left. I thought maybe he was doing that to compare my right with my left, since the cancer was on my right. He couldn't find anything on the left side either because there was never anything on the left. Dr. Jella went back to my right side of the chair. Lifted my right arm again and began feeling for the stone like lumps in my armpit, right side of my breast and rib cage area.

Again, he couldn't feel anything.

He became more puzzled and amazed; the thought had to have definitely entered his mind of: NOTHING! He moved around the chair to my left side again; began feeling the nodes on my left side once more: NOTHING. Next, we slightly lifted my bra and tank top to look and examine my left breast. Dr. Jella again felt my left breast for the tumors: NOTHING!

He stopped the exam, and while still standing at my left, he asked me, "Which side has the tumors?"

Excellent, he was stumped! The surprise I wanted was there! And I loved every moment!

Because he hadn't checked the file for the notes as to exactly where my cancer was before he began, he became unsure where I had been affected. I told him, "The tumors were on the right side." Dr. Jella moved around the chair again to my right side to examine my right breast, and again the nodes. The exam became more exciting for me. But; I still kept a straight face. It was a hard task because I already knew that the tumors were gone, and he didn't. The thrill of the appointment was worth keeping him and his nurse in the dark. I remember the excitement of that appointment as vividly as though it just happened today. I love you Dr. Jella, and everything you did for me, but I needed the exam to be honestly spontaneous.

Now he became excited and amazed because all he could feel was the cyst that I've had in my right breast for the past thirty-four years! That appointment was the first time I can remember seeing happiness and joy on his face!

Dr. Jella blurted out, "There had been only one chemo treatment! There is absolutely no way that there would have been any change whatsoever from one chemo treatment! There just is no way at all that there could have been any sign of stopping the growth rate! What are you doing?!"

Of course, I'm beaming from ear to ear same as the Cheshire Cat from *Alice in Wonderland*! When he gave me my prognosis, we were hoping the chemo would *hopefully only slow the growth* of tumor after twelve months of three-week cycles of chemo!

He had his nurse, Heidi, examine my right breast also because she was at the first appointment I had with Dr. Jella, when I went in with the tumors. With amazement and joy, she agreed that the tumors were no longer there! They were both shocked.

They both asked me again with amazement and shock, *"What are you doing?!"*

I started to remind them of past discussions we had regarding the visits with the oriental medicine doctor, Dr. Ron, who did the meridian balancing, a lot of prayer warriors praying and fasting for me across the country, along with watching my diet, and ...... he cut me off.

Said to me with a bit of humor, "Well, I want to think it was all me, my treatment that caused the change." Then with compassion and joy he said, "I'm very happy that you had such wonderful spiritual and prayer support. That's an important part of healing." He moved to his file and made some notes to my medical record. He decided to reduce the dosage a little.

I was surprised by his excitement, affirmation and gratitude that I had so much prayer going on for me at the time. I never saw him beam with so much joy. Before that day, he was so doom and gloom and very solemn about my prospects of surviving. A number of times he had told me that I had a "hundred percent likelihood of no cure or survival".

I knew that was part of the purpose with all of this happening to me. I was to prove a personally designed nutritional program, the complimentary therapies, along with spiritual attitude and prayer work.

The medical and complimentary therapies can do great things for humans and animals by working together; by the medical profession accepting that many of these alternative therapies have a lot of merit and should be incorporated into a treatment program to abide by Hypocrites' oath. Also, more of the health insurance companies need to include these therapies into what they accept for our health care and prevention of diseases. Seems to me it would be far less costly to provide for this type of coverage, than to wait until the disease occurs and have the major expenses of curing or controlling the disease. Also, the impact on the patient's viability for a quality life and career would be reduced. The person would remain more productive at work, home life, school, and.... It's all about the bottom line, is it not?

Thursday, September 4, 2008, 8:30 AM.   Follow-up appointment with my surgeon, Dr. Jewett.

Shelly, Jewett's nurse, came to get me from the waiting area. She was exuberantly happy to see me as she always was. I'm sure she greats all their patients with the same amount of joy. It's her nature. But I like to think I'm a little more special.

Shelly took my temp and blood pressure. Both were good. I was excited to tell her the news about my cure, but we talked about past events and the preliminary gibberish about why I was there; to have the surgeon check out the MediPort he inserted because I had had problems with it in July. I thanked her for sending me the *Thinking of You* card.

She commented that she was told that I had left for out West. I said, "No, had things to get organized yet, and had to get some money together. Besides," I said very calmly, "there had been a major development with my breast I felt I needed to stay to see how things develop. And I miss Mike too much unless I'm able to be with him for a few minutes out of the day, which is worse if I'm away for longer periods. Talking with him on the phone helps while I'm on a trip, but I'm usually eager to be back with him, unless he travels with me."

I commented that as a result of my miracle I was trying to come up with a way to spend more time with my kids out West, and Mike, my friends and family in the Midwest. We talked a little about snow birding, so that seemed to be an approach that might be worked on as I recover from the few times of chemo I had received.

Of course, Shelly needed to know how I was doing and what the major development was that had occurred to me, "What was the *miracle* you had just mentioned?" I started to tell her about my chemo appointment I had with Dr. Jella on August 15, 2008. She was very happy and excited about the good news, and said, "I have to tell Dr. Jewett that you've had some amazing results and you'll have to tell him your story! Is it OK that I tell him some of your story?" I nodded, "yes".

Shelly went to get Dr. Jewett and told him a little about our conversation as I waited for them to come back to the exam room. He said, "I hear there had been some developments?! What's going on?" So I started to explain the change with my breast and what happened at my appointment with Dr. Jella. About my miracle! Jewett was beaming with happiness to hear the good news!! His face lit up. It lit up even more to great excitement after telling him how I was led to using a number of alternative therapies, and how prayer was my greatest source of my cure.

He asked, "Would you mind putting on a gown so that I could examine you to see for myself?" I answered, "Absolutely, I was hoping you would do an exam." After giving me a few minutes to change clothes, Dr. Jewett returned with Shelly, and he started to check out the area of my underarm and breast, throat, and left side of my right breast. He couldn't feel any tumors either! He happily exclaimed, "WOW your breast is soft as it should be; not hard and large as it was before from the tumors!"

Standing at my right, Jewett helped me sit up from the exam table, and Shelly stood behind him with a huge smile on her face. They both were beaming with delight. He sat down at his little desk in the exam room to finish his notes on his "Patient Instruction Sheet" attached to his clip board. I noticed that he wrote – **"Doing Well! --Responding to Therapy (Alternative and +/- medical)! -- Port OK now, and – Exam: great!"**

He asked me to get dressed as he was preparing to head out of the room and requested that he wanted to see me again after my next chemo! He asked if there was anything else, and I shook my head to indicate "no".

After the door of the room closed, I could hear Jewett and Shelly talking. I could hear him excitedly tell Shelly through the door, "In all my thirty years as a doctor and surgeon, I had heard of numerous stories of things like this, but this was the first time I had ever seen one personally!" I *was very* happy to hear his comment. It made my day more than you can imagine!

His report stated that he examined me, and he was very impressed that he could not feel any definite mass under my arm, and the tumor in my breast had clearly gotten smaller. He also wrote that this change apparently occurred prior to getting the chemotherapy. He wrote that I had done multiple alternative therapies, but certainly prayer seemed to be the primary cause of the difference at this point. He stated again in his report that he was quite impressed with the current situation, and that I was doing great and in excellent spirits.

It wasn't until this appointment that I learned that the tumors in my right breast didn't only bend one biopsy needle when they did the biopsy. It had bent *three* needles that day! Shelly said, "Your tumor was so hard that I could hear the needles going into the tumor. The needles sounded as though they were going into a fossil-like material!" I exclaimed, "WOW! I'm impressed! I couldn't recall hearing the needle making that kind of noise. I must have been a little too groggy from the anesthesia that I only could remember seeing the needle they showed me during the biopsy. That needle was bent forty-five degrees!" We both talked more about being shocked about the bent needles from the biopsy, and for me to hear that information and learn that the tumor was as hard as a rock. I had no concept that my cancer was at that level that my doctors were amazed!

I think that Drs. Jella and Jewitt were surprised and frustrated at me not accepting their words of the diagnosis, that I remained happy, and up-beat throughout the process. I think they were more perplexed by my fighter mentality, my sense of purpose about this all, and my attitude of *I just knew that I was going to survive and live for many more years.* My attitude that I firmly believed in my heart and soul that God had plans for me for years to come, because He told me in two of the prayer sessions I had with others that spoke in tongues, that I should believe Him and what He told me.

Also, my conversation with Victoria confirmed what occurred in these two prayer sessions, as well as what I sensed myself. So I knew deep down that I just needed to find out how to fix the problem with which I was diagnosed. My purpose to find the source of what had caused it all, and to take better maintenance care of my temple body.

My directive, if you wish, was how to fix what had gone wrong, not cut away (remove) the symptom, not drug away the symptom, and definitely believe the doctors' diagnosis about me of zero percent survival was changeable and not permanent.

The chemo treatment was only an added step to my miracle because the chemo treatments were done after the tumor disappeared. It was the prayers and spiritual support which made me hear God's message and felt His guidance towards my miracle; it was the chi energy balancing of the meridians I had done; the graviola I took; the personally designed nutrition and herbal program; and finally my commitment and attitude to discover my means of survival and miracle God had laid out for me.

I followed His g-u-i-dance.

These were the methods that provided most of the cure. Primarily these resources were the means to my cure and miracle; not the chemo. Ultimately, my apparent need of the medical doctors was the type of documentation it provided to know what I was up against, some of the emotional support given me by the doctors and nurses, of which I am eternally grateful, and quite certainly the behemoth of a need to blend the two methods of medically aiding people in their quest towards as perfect health as possible until our day comes to pass on.

July and August of 2010, my beloved doctors put me through the whole regimen of tests again to make sure the cancer had stayed away. I had the PET Scan again which showed *everything as all clear*, three MRI's which also showed nothing, and my cancer antigen level was again at the 20.0 range. Still cancer free. I am so grateful to God, Jesus, Mike, Sue, Dr. Jella, Dr. Jewett, Dr. Choi, Marcia, Dr. Ron, Kanelechi, Ruth, and all of those who cared, supported and prayed for me through this journey.

Keep in mind that the Bible states in Genesis that God said everything our bodies need to keep it healthy and to heal it are in our plant life. Also, I had been using herbs since my kids were babies and used to grow and dry herbs. We have always had better results and fewer side effects with herbs.

Therefore, I used the saliva swab test to learn what my chemical makeup was before the first chemo treatment. I wanted to know what my body was doing before the chemo cycles began. The saliva tests were performed during the chemo to monitor my progress. I continue to do the saliva test at least quarterly, and as needed to monitor my body (sort of like an oil change), or after an out of routine period of time due to a trip or event where I may have compromised the stability of my personal program to keep my body on its rapidly healing path as well as avoid ever having cancer again.

The saliva test helps to determine how to *fix the source of the problem, not only the symptom.* I believed the solution to my dilemma was in what I was consuming, and I needed to find out exactly how to correct what I was doing wrong.

Thank You, Jesus. I'm so grateful that You had guided me towards those that would be able to help me and provide the quick cure you wanted me to have!

Without a doubt, God had been choreographing my life for years to this point.

As I reflected back over that part of my life, numerous events were pulled out to help me put together *Being Held By God.* In 2005, I was told by a believing person that I would be writing a book. I remembered that prediction, but at the time I questioned the validity and likelihood of it ever happening! I couldn't think of anything worthy of writing about and didn't think I was capable of writing a book.

HA! Here we are.

I've written *Being Held By God* to you, and you're reading that "book". If you don't have faith in God, the intelligent designer; and follow His **g-u-i-dance** in your dance with Him the world will come up and bite you in the butt!

Many blessings to you to achieve
all the desires God had given you!

With God, all things are possible!

DANCE WITH JESUS!

Appendix A

Chronology

December 2007	**Phone call** from Doris
January 2008	**1st message** from God through Doris and Carl re Marcia Simler and Dr. Ronald Wagner
March 2008	**Bruise** appeared on right breast
April 2008	**Inflammation** appeared on right breast
April 2008	**Took antibiotics** for inflammation
April 2008	**2nd message** from God through Katherine re Marcia Simler
May 19, 2008	**Mammogram** - nurses told me to go immediately to see primary doctor **Branding** with "cancer"
May 27, 2008	**Victoria Bullis** conversation
May 29, 2008	**Breast Biopsy** - Dr. Bryan Jewett **Started Therapy with Dr. Ron Wagner and 3rd Message from God** re Marcia Simler
May 2008	**Mel Simonovich** told me about graviola
June 4, 2008	**Cancer Antigen Blood Test** (CA 27.29) result is 58.4, Normal is 0-40.
June 10, 2008	**CT Scan** 9:30 am at the Hartford Clinic

	of the chest, pelvic, and abdomen
June 16, 2008	**Graviola (N-Tense) Arrived**
June 18, 2008	**PET CT Scan**
July 7, 2008	**12:30 AM Surgical Placement of the MediPort** and CT-guided biopsy of the liver lesion.
July 15, 2008	**Call from Kathy, God's 4th messenger** re Marcia Simler **Called Marcia Simler** to learn how she could help me Started **Type A nutrition** and **alkalizing body**
July 17, 2008	**Marcia sent ZetaMax & saliva kit**
July 18, 2008	**Dr. Jella's last exam before chemo** **MediPort failed to flush** **Sent to Hartford Hospital** to examine cause of MediPort failure **Returned to Clinic** – hospital couldn't test me Clinic sent me home – chemo rescheduled for July 21, 2008
July 19, 2008	**Saliva sample mailed** to Marcia Simler, Natural Health Works, for my **first saliva test**
July 21, 2008	**Scan and x-rays of MediPort** at hospital because the MediPort wasn't working - chemo rescheduled for July 25, 2008
July 22, 2008	**Prayer with Kanelechi** and her friend

July 23, 2008	**Tumor reduced by ½ the size**
July 24, 2008	**Tumor reduced by ½ the size again**
July 24, 2008	**First saliva results received**
July 25, 2008	**No tumor in breast**
July 25, 2008	**Friday First Chemo appointment 10:00 AM – 3:50 PM - Friday, at Vince Lombardi clinic in Slinger.** No Dr. Jella
July 28, 2009	Monday morning received **first shipment of supplements** from Marcia.
August 15, 2008	**8:38 AM Friday, Second Chemo and surprise exam** of disappearance of tumors. Dr. Jella report: The right breast lump has significantly decreased to the point that it is hard to get the margins now or good size estimate per se. I do not appreciate any right axillary adenopathy which was very obvious prior to first cycle of chemo.
August 29, 2008	**2nd Saliva Test** with Marcia Simler
September 4, 2008	**Dr. Jewett,** miracle exam and conversation
September 5, 2008	**Third Chemo**. **Blood drawn today for cancer antigen: down to 30.9,** Normal is 0-40
September 26, 2008	**Fourth Chemo**
October 17, 2008	**Fifth Chemo**

November 7, 2008   **Sixth Chemo**
November 17, 2008 **3rd Saliva Test** With Marcia Simler
December 1, 2008   Friday, Dr. Jella appointment. No more
                   chemo
December 17, 2008 12:15 pm, Wednesday Slinger, WI
                   PET Scan. Complete resolution

Appendix B

Contributors and Sponsors of *Being Held By God* and Cancer Survivor Hands 4 Hope, a 501C(3) for cancer survivors to restart and rebuild their lives after cancer:

Rose Mary Pies
Joy Kuhnke
Susan Strahl and Robert Serwe
Michele and Ronald Genske
Michael and Ruth Koenig
Jean Commons
Richard Green, CPA
Rita and Roy Watring
Theresa and Joseph Soriano
Theresa Wysocki
Sally Fischer
Andrea Stewart
Kristin Wisely
Bryan Jewett, MD
Shelly Markus, MA
Ann Langenfeld Smith
Kanelechi Kamah

Resources

Nannette Jodar
is available to speak at your organization, church or company. If you would like to contact me for additional resources, you may reach me through my:

Email: jodarmiracle@gmail.com.
Twitter: www.twitter.com/nannettejodar
Facebook: www.facebook.com/BeingHeldByGod
Website: www.nannettejodar.com

Marcia Simler
Certified Natural Health Practitioner
Herbalist and Kinesiologist
Natural Health Works, LLC
W4745 Blumer Road
Monroe, WI 53566
Phone: 800-753-1689
Email: angels4@tds.net
www.naturalhealthworksonline.com

Marcia Simler is the Herbalist and Kinesiologist who did my saliva test and still does today. Marcia Simler is the owner of clinic in Monroe, Wisconsin, called Natural Health Works, LLC, and certified in kinesiology, and for over 22 years of experience. Kinesiology is a tool that uses the muscles to find the imbalances in your body. Kinesiology is somewhat like acupuncture, only non-invasive techniques that find the imbalances, deficiencies, and what the body requires to heal itself. It takes the guessing out of what your individual body needs, and pinpoints what will balance the body. She checks the functioning percentage of your organs, how well your systems are working, along with what you need to cleanse and detoxify. Marcia checks the types of vitamins, minerals, and herbs which will balance your deficiencies. "Are you sick and tired of being tired?" is her logo, and she loves to share her knowledge to get each person their personally designed health nutritional plan for their body type, and what are they missing of the 60 minerals, 28 vitamins, and 3 essential fatty acids, and 12 amino acids the body needs each day.

Dr. Ronald Wagner
419 Baitinger Ct,
Sun Prairie, WI 53590-1544
608-695-1881
Email: roncwagner@gmail.com
www.healingenergy.net

- Dr. Ron used Common Sense with Natural Holistic Healing Arts

- His therapies included Angel Wing Kinesiology with Body & Mind Kinetic Integration, this is Unwinding Physical, Mental, Emotional Energy Blocks, and Cellular Memory
- He also used Kinesiology Bodywork, Range of Motion Extremity Unwinding, Pelvic, Spinal, & Cranial Unwinding, Joint Tension Release with Gentle Tui Na (Tuina), CSF Energy Wave
- With the Oriental Healing Arts, he used Meridian Therapy, Magnetic Touch, Surround the Dragon, Acupuncture Tonification Points to balance the excess and deficient meridians. When holding points, he used Qi Kong (Chi Gong) Visualization and Creative Positive Thinking
- To remove body congestion, he created and developed the Painless Intercellular Lymphatic Drainage Chi Energy Massages With the Possibility of Reduction or Removal of Intercellular Fluids, Congestions, and Cellulite

Victoria Bullis
Psychic and Metaphysical Healer
    She is located in California and London, England
    Website: www.victoriabullis.com
    Twitter: www.twitter.com/victoriabullis.com

Raintree Nutrition, Inc.

Raintree Nutrition is where I purchased the product N-Tense version of graviola, and still do today.

3579 Hwy 50 East, Suite 222

Carson City, Nevada 89701   U.S.A.

To Order: 800-780-5902   8:00 AM to 4:00 PM PST

Customer Service & International Calls:

775-841-4142

Email: info@rain-tree.com

www.rain-tree.com

Nature's Sunshine

800-223-8225

International: 801-342-4578

www.naturessunshine.com

Dr. Bryan Jewett, MD

Physician, General Surgeon

Aurora Health Center Hartford, Wisconsin

Aurora Health Center Slinger, Wisconsin

Aurora Health Center West Bend, Wisconsin
    Education:

Geargetown University School of medicine in
    Washington, DC

Cleveland Clinic Foundation in Cleveland, OH

Dr. Abhay Jella, MD

Medical Oncology/Hematology and Internal Medicine

Aurora Health Center

Vince Lombardi Cancer Clinic, Slinger, Wisconsin
    53086
Education:
Osmania Medical College in Hyderabad, India
Michael Reese Hospital in Chicago, Illinois
University of Iowa Hospitals & Clinics in Iowa City,
    Iowa